ENDOP SE

Gloria Ashby has written one of the [barcode: D0851349] als I have ever read. She takes you on a journey a. ... . spiritual dots in your life together. You can't put it down. ... . it will encourage you to live your life at a different level.

Liz Morris, The Personality Doctor and President,
The Dallas Dream Team

Gloria Ashby has a way with thoughts, words, and insights. Her unique approach to this devotional helped me "connect the dots" in my life. Her stories are entertaining, yet profound, as they help the reader to connect the dots with God and others. I highly recommend it!

Donna Skell, Executive Director of Roaring Lambs Ministries

This book is so clear, real, and compelling. Gloria never fails to be transparent and to encourage me to go deeper into God's Word. Her word pictures beautifully illustrate the lessons she has learned from her walk with Lord. They are memorable and inspiring.

Pat Gordon, Board Member of CBMC International, Board of Directors Member
and Senior Vice President of The Dallas Dream Team, Speaker and servant leader,
Stonecroft Ministries

Collaborating with Gloria on several large-scale, change-management projects, I witnessed first-hand the powerful influence of her privately held spiritual beliefs in a complex business environment. She infused our work with guidance that led to the cultural changes needed to create and sustain the positive business results we sought. Gloria's words and actions consistently demonstrate her desire to make the world a better place. She is an inspiring leader and writer who knows our inner voice makes us who we are. *Connecting the Dots* is an enjoyable read that supports and encourages all of us to embrace the true purpose of our collective human journey.

Pamela Bond, Retired Vice President, Fidelity Investments, Inc.,
Author of "The Authenticity Compass"

God presented Gloria Ashby with the ministry of words. She is always able to put a profound thought together. Her words will inspire, encourage, and teach those who want to grow in a deeper walk with the Lord. What a great gift her devotional *Connecting the Dots* will be.

Rosemary Legrand, Director of Operations,
Christian Literary Awards, Joy and Company

CONNECTING
the
DOTS

Learning to Live a Word-Shaped Life

GLORIA K. ASHBY

Connecting the Dots
Learning to Live a Word-Shaped Life
Gloria K. Ashby

To contact the author:
email: gloriaashby.connectingdots@gmail.com

Published by:

Mary Ethel Eckard
Frisco, Texas

ISBN (Print): 978-1-7357853-2-5
ISBN (E-book): 978-1-7357853-3-2

For my precious granddaughters,

Felicity Kate

and

Daisy Quinn

CONTENTS

Section 3. | Somebody Should've Said Something

Section 4. | Learn to Lead Like Jesus

Section 5. | Faith Words To Grow By

SECTION 6. | CHOICES

SECTION 7. | AGING TO PERFECTION

SECTION 8. | THE NEXT STEP

APPENDIX

INTRODUCTION

"We're each just a dot. I'm a dot, you're a dot. God told me to stand down. Let Him connect the dots."

One woman's discovery and words sucked all other thoughts and words out of the room. Our study group grew silent, letting this insight and wisdom sink into our souls.

Like many of the women seated in a circle to grow deeper in our walk with the Lord, I am a doer, particularly a completer-finisher. Give me a task and I will make it happen. All of it. Leave me alone unless I ask for help.

My lifelong battle cry, "I can do it myself." (Is it any wonder that was the title to my daughter's favorite Sesame Street book when she was five years old?) I charge forward and push to connect all the dots myself. I organize resources; outline deadlines and process steps to get to goal, and jump start the effort. I'll give hands-on support when needed as well as encourage and coordinate everyone involved, whether they like it or not. In the end, I will step in to put on finishing touches and declare, "Mission accomplished."

Then, I report for duty for the next assignment.

God made me this way, or so I thought. That day, the woman's words pierced me. They plunged me into considering a new way of thinking about myself – a dot in a bigger picture – and how I work as a dot.

I'm a dot. Everyone is a dot. Stand down. Let God connect the dots.

These words shifted how I live as God's beloved child and into His promises as a follower of Christ.

I am a dot. You're a dot.

In 1886 Georges Seurat developed a new technique for painting, called pointillism. Instead of brush strokes, he created masterful pieces of art by placing small but distinct dots of color on the canvas to form an image. Look closely at one of his or other dot paintings, and discover that each dot, because done by hand, is unique. Though some look similar, each is different in shape, size, color, or intensity of tone.

I am one of the many unique dots in our Creator's painting. God put in me, different than you, a set of passions, qualities, experiences, abilities, and skills in varying levels. All together, these make up my unique persona. Yours make up your unique persona. We may look or behave similarly to each other, but no two individuals are exactly alike.

The canvas God is painting on stretches from the beginning to the end of time when His Son, Jesus Christ, returns. And He knows what the finished painting looks like in minute detail. Thus, my Creator knows when, where, and how best to use my dot. He knows where and how my passions, qualities, abilities, experiences, and skills best carry out His ultimate purpose – that is, to reconcile all of humankind to Himself. To that end, He has placed me just so on the canvas.

My role in the picture is only this: to live as the unique dot God created me to be in the places where He puts me. I serve the Lord as Creator, allowing Him, His Word, and Holy Spirit, to define and color who I am in relationship with the other "dots" He places around me.

God takes care of the final pictures' outcome. I need only do what I can with who I am to serve in the capacity and place to which He calls me.

Stand down. Let God connect the dots.

While I am a dot with a particular purpose in the picture, I am not the Painter. Nor am I the full picture. Neither can I accomplish anything apart from the power of His Holy Spirit within me (John 15:5).

From my little spot on the canvas of life, I will never see the whole big picture God is creating. I touch only the five to seven dots around me. From that vantage point, I doubt that I see what is going on more than two to seven dots beyond me. I may sense what is forming in my corner of the world and time, but not further and not in detail. And certainly not days, weeks, or years down the road.

Trouble comes when I don't stand down but work to connect the dots myself. In those moments I can wind up connecting dots never meant to be connected, rushing ahead only to connect them incorrectly, or not connecting them at all when they were meant to be. During these times, I usually am impulsively working in one of four modes: FIDI (fix it/do it), FOMO (fear of missing out), or FTL (failure to listen), and FTA (failure to act). As Oswald Chambers warned, when we launch out under our own steam and agenda rather than God's, we run the risk of "making difficulties that will take years of time to put right."[1]

I know. Been there, done that.

Our Father-God is the Painter. He is always at work, connecting the dots. He paints to make "…everything to work together for the good of those who love God and are called according to his purpose for them … and … *to become like his Son*" (Romans 8:28-29, NIV).

This and our relationship with Him for all eternity is His goal. Our loving God speaks through His Word. His Word shapes life throughout history. All things serve this ultimate end.

Read out loud and hear God's promise to Isaiah:

> *... the words I speak.*
> *They will not return to me empty.*
> *They make the things happen that I want to happen,*
> *And they succeed in doing what I send them to do.*
> Isaiah 55:11 (NCV)

The Apostle Paul realized the implications of these words. He got how God worked when he wrote his letter to the Romans:

> *I pray I will be allowed to come to you, and*
> *this will happen if God wants it.*
> Romans 1:10 (NCV)

God, our Creator, weaves the web of events, linking people across time. He will connect the dots until His picture of the new Earth is complete. That is the good everything works towards – for us to be like His Son and with Him in eternity. He's the One putting us, His beloved dots, on the canvas. He's the one with the eternal vision, the One who connects us with His Word where needed to do what He needs us to do in that place.

The solution to FIDI, FOMO, FTL, and FTA tendencies: Stand down. Lead a Word-shaped life. Paint over messes, mistakes, and our self-absorbed maneuverings with the Holy Spirit. Color every moment of our life and world with His Word.

His Word, the Bible, is God's personal letter communicating to us His character, thoughts, instruction, and activity. If we listen for His Voice, He will speak to us personally through His Word. If we wait and watch, He surely sends "...the Helper, the Holy Spirit, whom the Father will send in my [Jesus] name, and who will teach you all things and remind you of everything that I have told you" (John 14:26, NIV).

Purpose of This Book

An autostereogram is a type of dot picture in which, if you stare at it long enough in a cross-eyed fashion, a three-dimensional scene forms within the two-dimensional image on the surface. The more I concentrated over time on God's words in scripture, the more those two-dimensional dots of His Word connected to form a three-dimensional autostereogram in my life.

The stories in this book reflect key moments and milestones in which God's Spirit connected the dots of His Word to my day-to-day experiences. The more I read and studied, the more His story became my story. The more those two-dimensional words on the page transformed into messages with a 3-D(eeper) personal meaning for my experiences, behavior, and circumstances.

Some connections taught me a lesson. Others revealed God's nature or a bigger picture in the making. Still others showed or helped me become a better dot, a Christ-like dot, the one Our Father-Creator intended me to be on the grand canvas of His creation story. And forgive me if two stories appear to share a similar theme. That means I probably did not get it the first time God connected the dots for me or I slipped back into an old habit. All of them, however, moved me closer to living a 3-D, Word-shaped life.

By putting these stories on paper, I hope they help you, the reader, also lead a Word-shaped life. I pray they resonate and inspire you to see where God has been or is working on your beloved dot. So, take a moment. Stand down. And let God connect your dots.

Gloria K. Ashby

SECTION 1

. . . . . . 🪶 . . . . .

SURROUNDED BY
A GREAT CLOUD
OF WITNESSES

1
THE WOMEN IN ME

· · · · · · · ● ● ● ◉ ● ● ● · · · · · ·

Generations of women crowd inside me.

There's a carpenter, a seamstress, and a gardener squeezed beside a hairdresser, a bookkeeper, a caretaker, and a homemaker.

Women who worked long hours. Mom balanced managing four kids running in different directions, working part-time, and re-planting the family every time Dad's work called him to a different city. Her mother toiled in the fields of a farm, and ironed others' clothes to earn extra pennies for her family of eight. Dad's mom worked inside the home. She corralled two sons and later nursed an invalid husband after his stroke, and then nursed her second husband through pancreatic cancer.

None went to college. They weren't the deepest thinkers, but they encouraged me to think deeply. One had a heart for praise music and considered those from the church as family. Another had a passion gathering people around the table for hearty meals.

All outlived their husbands and fought anyone who messed with their children. Each passed on legacies of fierce independence — even during times when a woman's strong-mindedness was frowned upon or misunderstood.

All were survivors. All persevered and trusted God to deliver them through their circumstances.

Mom did
> — even while she battled persistent pain that came with health problems.

My maternal grandmother did
> — even when she bore the loss of an adult son to cancer.

My paternal grandmother did
> — even when age and health issues forced her to endure her final days in a skilled nursing facility.

All these mothers crowd inside me. Banding together, as women will do, to whip me into shape. To encourage me to embrace the person of faith the Lord created *me* to be.

CONNECTING THE DOTS

Remember the women of faith in our lives. We can stand on their shoulders as we recall how they faced weakness, poverty, and difficulties. And, like these women, our lives can do likewise for others.

These women are the mothers, grandmothers, friends, and co-workers, as well as women of the Bible and history. They nurture in us a legacy through how they lived day to day, how they carried themselves through times of plenty and times of little, finding their greatest joy, strength, and peace in the Lord.

> The lives of these women exemplify for us that
> we, too, can trust the Lord
> in whatever capacities He equips us,
> with whatever resources He gives us,
> and in whatever circumstances He leaves us.

*I have been reminded of your sincere faith, which first lived
in your grandmother Lois and in your mother Eunice and, I
am persuaded, now lives in you also. For this reason, I remind
you to fan into flame the gift of God, which is in you.*
2 Timothy 1:5-6 (NIV)

2

FAVORITES[1]

· · · · · · ● ● ● ● ● ● 🔘 ● ● ● ● ● ● · · · ·

At last, I'm escaping home. It's Friday night, and Daddy is driving me to Grandma's for my almost-weekly ritual of spending the weekend with her. All by myself. No little brothers distracting her with their antics. No baby sister cooing sweetly to be cuddled.

Just me ... nine years old, and skinny as a rail with stringy brown hair that falls into my eyes. I wear shorts, a top that slips off my shoulder and my first pair of glasses. Dark brown-rimmed and thick lenses because I am horribly near-sighted. Although I now see more clearly, the glasses are just one more thing I don't like about myself. But that doesn't matter tonight — because I'm going to Grandma's, and she likes my glasses.

Plus, she loves me best of all. I know because she whispered it to me once, cupping her hand to my ear so no one else heard. "You're my favorite, you know, because you're my first grandchild. You're special."

Going to Grandma's is like running away from home. Carrying my change of clothes in a paper grocery sack, I arrive at her three-room apartment where she lives since Grandpa died. We hug hello, though I can barely reach my arms around Grandma's waist. She's a high-calorie cook — and it shows.

I push Daddy out the door. Now my escape is complete from where I feel out of place and have no privacy, where I try to please Mama — but manage to draw an exasperated look at something I say, or get underfoot as she cleans up messes left by my brothers or sister or dog.

At last, I sigh and begin my weekend adventure where Grandma will let me be whoever I want and do whatever I want.

"Want something to eat?" she asks.

"Yes, let's play restaurant." I scrounge through the table drawer to dig out the order book Grandma bought me. With a stubby pencil poised over the paper, I stand by Grandma seated at her grey, Formica-topped dining table.

"What would you like, ma'am?" I ask, using my grown-up voice.

"Hmm," she puts her finger to her cheek and taps it as if deciding what delicious feast she fancies today. "I'll have vegetable soup, a cheese sandwich and sweet tea with a slice of lemon." I scribble her order, poke the pencil behind my ear like the truck-stop waitress I imagine I am, and walk to the stove to prepare the fare.

While the soup warms, I take two more orders from imaginary customers and pull dishes off open shelves above the sink. Grandma lets me use her good dishes as long as I'm careful not to drop them and return them clean at the end of my shift.

"Lunch is scrumptious," she exclaims, nibbling her sandwich. When she leaves, I notice she left me a tip -- two dimes that I sweep into my apron pocket.

Grandma retreats to her bedroom to freshen her makeup and grab her purse. She hollers out, "I need a few things from the dime

5

store. Wanna go?" That's code for "I'll buy you a treat." I'm at the door before she finishes her sentence.

We pile into her '53 Nash, hit the locks and cruise down the road with Elvis Presley blaring through the speakers, "I just wanna be ... your teddy bear ..."

At the dime store, Grandma buys me two books, *Black Beauty* and *Heidi*. She knows how I bury my nose in a book every chance I get. Back at the apartment, I curl up on her sofa. My world fades into another, and I am now Heidi visiting her grandfather in the Swiss Alps.

Grandma interrupts my frolic through the mountains only to hand me a bowl with five scoops of our favorite — vanilla ice cream. She takes a seat beside me. I drift back to the Alps while Grandma gently strokes my back, soothing me to sleep.

It's Friday night, fifteen years later. I drive past Grandma's old apartment and pull into her new driveway for my weekly visit. Grandma remarried — a man she met while out dancing at the county line with her girlfriends. She now lives in a two-bedroom house in one of the city's older neighborhoods, only five minutes from where I bowl in a league.

I plop down on her couch and ramble about my week. I feel nine years old again. Grandma sits beside me and gently strokes my back, soothing away my day's pressures.

"You need a bite before you go," she insists.

"I'm not that hungry, Grandma."

"Okay, I'll fix you just a bite." I hear the clanging of dishes and remember my waitress days in her apartment. The refrigerator door opens and shuts four or five times.

"Only a bite, Grandma," I remind her from the living room.

"Yes, just a bite. It's ready."

I enter the kitchen to find the grey, Formica-topped table hidden beneath a banquet of dishes. There's meatloaf, leftover fried chicken, and slices of Wednesday's roast beef surrounded by bowls of snap peas, new potatoes, corn on the cob, green salad, sliced tomatoes, and diced pineapple. She sees me roll my eyes. "It's just a bite," she objects. "Sit and eat."

I do as I'm told and build a sampler plate of the feast laid before me. Stuffed to the gills, Grandma polishes me off with a bowl of our favorite — vanilla ice cream.

I help her clear the table and toss scraps into the trash under the sink. That's when I discover something new about Grandma. Tucked in a corner and partially hidden from view is a bottle of Jack Daniel's Black Label. The surprise must register on my face because before I can ask, she answers, "Hush up. It's for medicinal purposes. Just one jigger a week helps my arthritis."

It's Saturday, another twenty years later. I roll up the nursing home's driveway for my weekly visit with Grandma. She came here under protest. Her frail body, weak with advancing dementia and depression from losing her husband, betrays her independence. Last week I took her out for our favorite — vanilla ice cream. Today, I bring her something different.

She sits in her wheelchair, staring at the television in her room. I slip into a chair beside her and stroke her back, soothing away her anxieties.

"Grandma, I have a surprise for you."

Her tired eyes turn toward me, "What is it?"

I pull a glass and a can of Coke from my tote. Then I slide out a bottle of Jack Daniel's Black Label. "For your arthritis." I wink at her, mix a jigger-full with Coke and hand her the glass.

Grandma's face brightens with memories. She raises the glass for a toast, drains it, and smiles at me. "You're my favorite, you know, because you're my first grandchild. You're special."

I return her smile. "And you're my favorite too, Grandma. You're more special than you know."

CONNECTING THE DOTS

God loves us unconditionally and without limits. He sends us Grandmas and Grandpas to spoil us just as He wants to spoil us with His love and blessings. We are each His "favorite." We are each special in His eyes.

... I am convinced that neither death nor life, nor angels nor rulers, nor things present nor things to come, nor powers, nor height nor depth, nor anything else in all creation, will be able to separate us from the love of God in Christ Jesus our Lord.
Romans 8:38-39 (NIV)

3

A HANDFUL OF LOVE

I noticed her hands first. Gnarled and rough like the twisted oak that shaded her front yard. Knuckles swollen with arthritis and reddened from years of hand washing clothes and scrubbing floors with ammonia and water.

My grandmother's wrinkled hand opened the screen door to greet Mama and me, her six-year-old granddaughter. She rushed us indoors before swarming flies could intrude.

I lugged my bag of clothes and books to occupy me through the weekend. I tossed them on the bed nestled in the living room on the wall opposite the camel-back couch — Mama Walker's answer to a guest suite in her three-room, shotgun-styled home in East Dallas.

The room smelled like musk from the coffee can of water perched on top of the space heater to moisten the dry, cold air. Wood floors creaked as I walked to stand by my grandmother.

"Be good and we'll pick you up Sunday afternoon," Mom announced, hugging her mother and waving goodbye to me.

Mama Walker's hands, wise with time, closed and double-locked the door. She turned and asked, "Wanna help me make fried apple pies?"

My mouth watered at the possibility of a rare treat Mom never made. I followed Mama Walker through the middle room to her kitchen at the back of the house. Her crooked fingers deftly tied a bib apron around my waist. I tucked my six-year-old fingers into the blue calico print's two front pockets. They were hand-sewn with uniform stitches despite her arthritic hands.

I climbed onto the seat of a step stool at her metal square table, where Mama Walker's hands would work their magic. "How much flour, Mama Walker?"

"Oh, a couple of handfuls."

She added a couple of her own after my handfuls left a puny amount in the bottom of the bowl.

"How much sugar?" I asked.

"About a handful. Enough to make it lightly sweet."

This time my handful was enough.

Mama Walker's hands reached for the apples. I stared at the adeptness with which her bent fingers guided the knife to pare the skin away, leaving perfect spirals to drop to the table. Then she sliced and chopped. Her hands added more sugar. Fingers pinched cinnamon. Palms mixed the ingredients.

Once cooked to soften and blend flavors, Mama Walker handed me a spoon to scoop the apple filling into the rounded dough. "Now fold the circle in half to cover the apples, and press the edges together," she instructed.

When my hands fumbled the pressed dough, Mama Walker reached out to cover mine with hers. Her hands, rough like fine sandpaper against my six-year-old skin, gently guided mine to form the pocket, into which they spooned the apples. Swollen knuckles and bent fingers lifted the pies into the skillet sizzling with oil.

Satisfied with a belly round and stuffed with fried apple pies and vanilla ice cream, I begged Mama Walker, "Please teach me to play your guitar."

For the next hour, Mama Walker's gnarled fingers slid across the guitar's strings with the ease and speed of a concert-ready classical guitarist. Mostly church songs, like *What a Friend We Have in Jesus* and *The Old Rugged Cross*. My fingers couldn't keep up, and the wire strings hurt where I pressed them to form a chord.

"You need to grow and get some calluses to toughen those fingers, Gloria."

I wasn't sure I wanted calluses. She must have noticed my frown because she suggested I would be a better quilter than a guitarist. "No calluses required there."

Again, roughened hands enfolded mine as Mama Walker showed me how to cut 3"x3" squares from her piles of scrap fabric. After lunch, they guided mine to stitch the squares together, feeding the fabric through the needle on her trestle sewing machine. I marveled at what straight seams came from her crooked fingers. "You can do it now," she said as she rose from the chair and motioned me to sit in her place.

After what seemed minutes, Mama Walker broke into my concentration on the whirring needle. "That's enough for a twin-sized quilt," she said, eying my stack of 3"x3" squares. "I'll quilt it for you next week."

Sunday morning. Mama Walker's hands ushered me out the front door. I felt every bend in her fingers as her white-lace, gloved hand grasped mine while we walked to the corner to catch the city bus, heading to the Gospel Lighthouse for church services.

Her hand never let go until we were seated in the large round auditorium and the music began. Both of my grandmother's gloved hands shot up high toward heaven in worship while her vibrato voice sang praises to the Lord.

This was a new experience for me … different from the reserved Methodist church of my father. Seeing others reach toward the sky, I, too, raised my hands and made a joyful noise in song, however off-key my untrained voice sounded. As the organ quieted, Mama Walker's hands lowered and lay still on her lap. Her twisted fingers intertwined one another, folded in quiet prayers of thanks.

Mama Walker's hands went still a final time while I was away at college.

As I passed the casket, her hands again drew my attention. The redness gone and gnarled fingers smoother, they rested on her stomach.

In that moment I grasped the handful of love Mama Walker poured into my life and that of those she met…this woman who divorced and remarried before traveling by covered wagon from Alabama to settle in Texas. This wife whose hands helped her husband scratch out a living on a small farm before needing to take in washing and ironing to keep food on the table after he lost his leg in an accident.

This mother who squirreled away pennies to buy her youngest daughter, my mother, a pair of coveted roller skates. This grandmother, whose gnarled and roughened hands impressed upon her granddaughter – me – what difference the gift of a handful of love can make to another.

CONNECTING THE DOTS

The Lord calls us to serve love as the hands and feet of Jesus in this world.

God showed His great love for us when He gave the gift of His only Son to die for us and free us from sin. It's our turn to give away this gift we first received – His love – by serving that same love to others, including the unloved, lost, and least of His children.

In the prayer of Teresa of Avila,

> *Christ has no body now but yours...Yours are the eyes through which he looks compassion on this world. Yours are the feet with which he walks to do good. Yours are the hands through which he blesses all the world. Yours are the hands, yours are the feet, yours are the eyes, you are his body. Christ has no body now on earth but yours.[2]*

Each one should use whatever gift he has received to serve others, faithfully administering God's grace in its various forms.
1 Peter 4:10 (NIV)

4

UNDER FATHER'S
WATCHFUL EYE

· · · · · · · · · ● · ● · ● · · · · · · ·

The fight was on.

The neighborhood tough shoved my brother in his chest and hurled mocking words to his face. The exchange escalated into a challenge to settle the disagreement with fists. Not one to back down from a fight, my brother threw off his jacket and stood firm, unafraid of his opponent. Friends who flanked the two foes now encircled them. The boys wrestled each other to the ground. Arms flailed and knuckles connected.

Dad, hearing commotion on his front lawn, walked to the door.

"Daddy, aren't you going to do something?" I whined, irritated by the noise and break in my concentration on a complicated math assignment.

"Not yet." He stood, quietly watching the two rivals. His hand rested on the doorknob, and he leaned forward slightly as if ready to charge through the door.

I forgot about my math problem and climbed up on the couch to grab a better view from the living room window.

When my brother gained the upper hand, one of the sideline toughs moved toward the fray to help his friend. Faster than a thoroughbred out of the starting gate, my father flew out the door and onto the front porch.

The young man caught Dad's presence out the corner of his eye. He hesitated. My father pointed his finger and commanded, "It'll be a fair fight. No ganging up. It's one on one!" The young man retreated.

My brother won the advantage. His opponent withdrew with bruises and broken glasses. He hobbled down the sidewalk, nursing his wounds. The two friends flanked either side. One glanced back as if considering a second attack. The wounded boy grabbed his friend's shoulder, "Let it go."

Just as we finished dinner later that evening, the doorbell rang. My father opened the door to find the defeated young man standing on the front steps with his dad. His dad confronted my father about what his son had described as an "unfair, unprovoked beating" and damages.

A small smile crept across the corners of my father's mouth. His eyes burned fiercely at the young man standing slumped beside his own father. Dad's voice firmly spoke the truth, "Your son was the one who came onto OUR property, instigated the argument, AND threw the first punch. I know because I was here when it happened."

The defeated young man cowered under his father's glare, "Is this true?" In a barely audible voice, the boy replied, "Yes."

His dad turned to my father. "Then I'm sorry to bother you." He turned to his son, "We'll talk again at home." The two men left.

CONNECTING THE DOTS

Watching my father guard and deliver my brother from the enemy reminded me that our heavenly Father stands up for us, too. Even in times of trouble we cause ourselves, I discovered He's there. Loving us. Delivering us through.

Edom, the enemy, delighted in Israel and Judah's misfortunes. Jealous of God's blessings upon them, Edom took advantage of their weakened state. But Edom underestimated the power of God, who promised – and would – judge harshly the nations who unfairly ganged up on His children.

Obadiah, the prophet, foretold how God, the Father, would stand up for His children. While Judah's sins provoked their fall, God still loved them. He stood ready to restore them once they returned to Him. All of us live under our Father's watchful eye.

You should not look down on your brother in the day of his misfortune, nor rejoice over the people of Judah in the day of their destruction, nor boast so much in the day of their trouble...The day of the Lord is near for all nations. As you have done, it will be done to you; your deeds will return upon your own head.
Obadiah: 12, 15 (NIV)

5

KEEP PEDALING[3]

Dad strolled out of the garage with a wrench in his hand while I biked up and down the sidewalk. He stopped at the end of our driveway and waved the wrench toward my training wheels. "You're ready to take those off."

I wasn't so sure. My six-year-old feet barely reached the pedals dad built up with wooden blocks on my new, 24" electric blue and silver Schwinn. As he unscrewed the bolts that attached the training wheels, Dad shot me a fatherly smile and said, "You got this. You can balance on your own now."

Training wheels tossed aside, we walked to the middle of the street. Mom stood at the opposite end, two house-lengths away. My sister, brother, and neighborhood friends lined the curb to watch me take flight or crash onto the pavement. I straddled the bike, just tall enough to peer over the handlebars.

"Ride straight toward Mom," Dad said. "I'll run beside you and hold the back of the seat until you get your balance. Ready?"

I took three deep breaths, put my right foot on the pedal, and pushed it forward. As the right pedal went down, my left foot caught the rising left block of wood. I pumped in a circular motion but wobbled, struggling to point the front wheel toward Mom.

As promised, Dad ran beside me, holding my seat to keep me balanced. Halfway to Mom, he let go. I panicked. I forgot to pedal, and the front wheel swerved wildly back and forth.

"Keep pedaling. Keep going. You're doing fine." Dad's words came from behind me.

I held the handlebars steady and pedaled with all my might. The front wheel stopped wobbling. I reached Mom and rode past her, grinning from ear to ear.

CONNECTING THE DOTS

Keep pedaling. The same powerful God who raised Jesus from the dead is the same Lord who trains and equips us with whatever we need to do whatever He calls us to do.

That bicycle memory pops to mind whenever I embark on something new — like stare into the face of a daunting challenge or ride into a new season of life. Like when I started a new school in a new city where we moved; when I no longer relied on parents for financial help, or switched career paths to answer my heart's passion, or retired. Each time I envisioned my father trotting by my side, reassuring me, "You're ready."

With each change – whether by choice, calling, or circumstance – I reach a crossroads in faith. Then, I hear my Father-God say, "You've practiced enough. Let's take those training wheels off."

Though I may wobble at first, His Holy Spirit reminds me, "You got this. Just keep pedaling."

Now may the God of peace who brought again from the dead our Lord Jesus, the great shepherd of the sheep, by the blood of the eternal covenant, equip you with everything good that you may do his will, working in us that which is pleasing in his sight...
Hebrews 13:20-21 (ESV)

6

THE POWER OF INVITATION

· · · · · · ●●● ● ●●● · · · · · ·

A former missions director, she embraced her new mission field. She entered last, rolling her walker behind two residents she gathered along the journey from her apartment to the chapel where our class met.

I welcomed my Andrew. Her real name was Jean, but I called her Andrew, after the disciple who brought others to Christ. Remember Andrew? The disciple who ran to find his brother, Simon, and said, "Come, I found the Messiah" (John 1:40-41). The one who later brought the young boy with five barley loaves and two fish to Jesus to feed 5,000 (John 6:5-9). The same disciple who helped a group of inquiring Greeks meet Jesus (John 12:20-22).

That was Jean. The one who, from the day I started teaching Bible study at the retirement community, invited people to come hear the Word. Jean and six residents greeted me that first Wednesday.

"This is everyone today, but others need to come," Jean said in her soft-spoken voice. Thus, began her mission to gather people the first and third Wednesday of each month.

Jean created and distributed flyers about class time and location. She table-hopped during lunch to remind the seniors when the day arrived. Jean knocked on doors of napping residents as time

> No contact equals no impact. No invite equals no possible influence.

approached and asked office help to announce class over the loudspeaker at the stroke of 4:30 p.m. If someone walked by after the lesson began, Jean called out to them. If they didn't hear her, she walked after them to pull them from the hallway into our meeting. Some came in; others resisted and declined.

Class attendance grew despite one last hurdle ... BINGO. Its schedule conflicted with Bible study. When only an "N39" away from a winning card, who looks at the clock? Or can pull themselves from the game?

"There's no reason we can't do both," Jean declared. Like the persistent friend who knocked on his neighbor's door at midnight (Luke 11:5-8), Jean lobbied residents and office staff to re-schedule BINGO. Three months later, 12-15 residents showed up for class. Before too many more weeks passed, our group grew to 18-20. So, I smile and give thanks for Jean and all *my* Andrews. Those who invited me to "Come, we have found the Messiah."

CONNECTING THE DOTS

Jean modeled the power of one who intentionally invites another into a faith conversation.

A person's decision to trust Christ is the climactic step that follows a series of smaller steps orchestrated by God to draw a person to Himself.[4] It is a process, not an event. Studies also show that a person who commits to follow Christ as an adult averages nine to twenty-five relationships or encounters with Christians before making that decision for themselves.[5] We rarely know for sure which encounter our invitation is – the first, seventh, twentieth, or twenty-seventh.

Likewise, growing as a follower of Jesus Christ is another series of steps after the conversion experience. The more we study and grow in relationship with Jesus, the more we become like him.

No contact equals no impact. No invite equals no possible influence. Our personal mission field is those we meet on a daily or one-time basis. There, we are all called to be missionaries, ambassadors for Christ (2 Corinthians 5:20). We only serve in different mission fields.

The challenge: who can we invite to "Come, we have found the Messiah"?

Andrew, Simon Peter's brother, was one of the two who heard what John had said and who had followed Jesus. The first thing Andrew did was to find his brother Simon and tell him, "We have found the Messiah" ... And he brought him to Jesus."
John 1:40-41 (NIV)

7

BEFRIENDING THE UNFRIENDED

· · · · · · · ● ● ● ● ● ◉ ● ● ● ● ● ● · · · ·

One afternoon, our daughter's eyes glistened with tears from a heart that ached for her classmate, Georgie.*

"Mom, they taunt him constantly," Jessica said. "Today they aimed spit wads and packages of jelly at the back of his head. When he turned around to see who threw that stuff, those boys just pestered him even more. They say mean things like, 'Georgie, you look like a rag doll on drugs,' or 'I bet you can't even tie your shoes.'"

Georgie was not the average boy. His speech impediment and stunted growth allowed for easy fault-finding. Unkempt, woody hair and scraggly fingernails provided the ideal target for pre-teen torture. While teachers adored his laugh and bright spirit, they, too, considered him "special."

Our daughter recognized Georgie was unlike other boys. When she first met him three grades earlier, she thought his life was easy... no homework, no tests, no assignments, and the school still promoted him year after year. Her perception changed after she witnessed the taunts he endured daily.

Pained from imagining today's episode, the only help I could offer was to ask a question. "Sweetie, do you remember when kids teased you?"

"Yeah, because I was skinny or got good grades. And when I started wearing glasses."

"Well, what stopped your tears and helped you get through that time?"

"My friends," she offered without hesitation. "They told me not to listen to those other kids. That they were the real losers. Jerks." She paused, lost in the memory. Suddenly her face brightened with an idea. "I'll just be what others won't... his friend."

A few days later, Jessica risked befriending the one who lived on the fringes in middle school. She strolled into class, assignment in hand, took her seat, and waved at Georgie sitting beside her. While he peered around the room, Jessica leaned over and whispered, "Georgie, did you write your speech for today?"

"What speech?" he replied.

"The one due today. About an important person in U.S. history," Jessica prompted him to remember.

Then, sounding hoarse and eyes widened with panic, Georgie whispered, "Jessica? Will you help me? With my speech?"

She paused for a second, then responded, "All right, but we must work quietly while others prepare too."

Georgie chose Martin Luther King as his subject. Amid hushed whispers of gawking twelve-year-olds, Jessica retrieved an encyclopedia for Georgie to use. She scooted her desk closer to his and coaxed Georgie, asking him questions to glean the main ideas in the passage. While Jessica prodded, Georgie chewed on his bottom lip, laboring to translate the article into his own words.

Prep time ended, and their teacher called the first student to deliver his speech. When Georgie's turn came, he offered Jessica a quick nod and smile of gratitude for her help. Georgie skipped to the podium and presented his oration, but absent his usual halting rhythm or stuttering over words.

"And in addeeshun to Mister King's many achievements, he was the Bapteest preacher who led Amereecan people to a new way of thinking. People learned to not judge others by the color of their skin, but by the content of their character. That is my report. Thank you."

Jessica's fellow student and friend offered a toothy grin to the audience and returned to his desk. He fidgeted, restraining himself from popping out of his chair to peer over the teacher's shoulder as she completed the critique sheet and recorded his grade. Finally, the teacher motioned Georgie forward. He darted to her desk.

"An eighty," he shouted with glee. "I didn't jus' pass, I did good." Laughter rippled through the classroom, but Georgie never noticed. He leveled his eyes on Jessica. His crooked smile thanked her again for pushing him to earn a grade higher than his obligatory seventy. Georgie bowed to the class and strutted back to his chair with a rare confidence.

While most students jeered Georgie's enthusiastic response to his grade, Jessica only smiled at her friend.

CONNECTING THE DOTS

Choose to love the unlovable. Befriend the unfriended. By doing so, who knows what rare courage and confidence will be unleashed in another.

Jesus showed deep affection for the unlovable, like the Samaritan woman at the well, the lepers, and the outcasts of society. He even took them into his inner circle and ministry, like Matthew the despised tax collector, or the uneducated fishermen – John, James, Peter, and Andrew. Christ's love and friendship for the lowly and those who lived on the edges of society, transformed their lives. They were never the same.

We have a choice. Love – or ignore, despise and reject – the unlovable. Befriend – or avoid – the unfriended. Our decision will make all the difference in the world.

Don't pick on people, jump on their failures, criticize their faults - unless, of course, you want the same treatment. Don't condemn those who are down; that hardness can boomerang. Be easy on people; you'll find life a lot easier. Give away your life; you'll find life given back, but not merely given back - given back with bonus and blessing.
Luke 6:37-38 (The Message)

*Not his real name.

8

SPA DAY

· · · · · · · ● ● ● ⬤ ● ● ● ● · · · · · ·

We can't fix some relationships this side of heaven. Yet, some we can. If we drop our guard, lay aside differences, and reach out with love.

Fridays were my day to stay with Mom, who suffered a chronic illness that stole her strength and much of her independence. I couldn't fix those physical problems, but I could make her more comfortable and give her a day to shine.

That Friday rolled around. I anticipated Mom's resistance to my idea since her weakened state only heightened her tendency toward self-sufficiency. That's why I took a deep breath and announced in my most affirmative voice, "We're going to have a spa day."

Mom squinted her eyes, shooting me a wary glance. "I've never done that."

"After today, you can't say that." I gave Mom my biggest grin, wiggled my eyebrows, and said, "You'll love it. I promise." Her squint relaxed. Mom leaned back in her recliner and smiled. I hurried to the bathroom for supplies before she could change her mind.

For the next hour, I gently washed her paper-thin skin and slathered lotion over her arms, hands, and legs. The Nike, Just-Do-It symbol on her socks beckoned next. "Mom, feet now. There's nothing like a foot rub. It's the next best thing to heaven if you ask me."

As I peeled off the right sock, a layer of dead cells fell like winter's dusting of snow onto the carpet. Placing her foot into my lap, I buffed the shedding skin. With four squirts of lotion, my fingers kneaded her heels and arches.

As I reached for her left foot, Mom asked, "Why are you going to all this trouble?" I am the oldest of her four children. And I am the one who inherited most of her fierce independence, perhaps borne out of her growing up during the depression. Over time, our dual penchant for self-determination left a gaping chasm between us.

"Why?" I answered. "Because you deserve it. To make you feel good ... special ..." Really why ... to close that gap between us. To draw her close. To make up for all the times my first-born, independent ways held her at arm's length. To open the door and heal wounds I caused through the years.

As I left that day, Mom's voice wrapped around my heart like a warm blanket. "I enjoyed you're being here so much," she said. "I appreciate everything you did. You're coming back next Friday, aren't you?"

We can't fix some relationships this side of heaven. Yet, some we can. If we drop our guard, lay aside differences, and reach out with love. For me and Mom, spa day was that day.

CONNECTING THE DOTS

Love never fails to fix what we break with our inadvertent or stubborn self-centeredness. Take the first step to restore relationships. Risk dropping the defensive guard. Forgive slights. Find common ground and reach out with love. Most people are doing the best they can anyway.

> *Love is patient and kind. Love is not jealous or boastful or*
> *proud or rude. It does not demand its own way. It is not*
> *irritable, and it keeps no record of being wronged. It does not*
> *rejoice about injustice but rejoices whenever the truth wins*
> *out. Love never gives up, never loses faith, is always hopeful,*
> *and endures through every circumstance. Love never fails.*
> 1 Corinthians 13:4-8 (NLT)

9

HOW LONG IS A GOOD LIFE?

A long life might not be good enough, but a good life is always long enough.

The pastor spoke these words to friends and family, who gathered to remember and mourn the loss of Marcus, a 29-year-old gentle giant of a man. His life was cut short on March 4th by a bullet fired in a senseless drive-by shooting.

The 6' 3" Tennessee Tech linebacker found Christ at fourteen years old and never stopped living his faith. He spoke words of encouragement to fellow workers, comforted the troubled, and offered acts of kindness for the challenged. Marcus adopted a fatherless five-year-old as his "little brother" and served as a role model in the young men's ministry.

As I packed his desk at work, I found one last note Marcus had written. "What do I want to do? Help others turn their potential into reality." Those few words summed up what those who knew him observed.

In his short life, Marcus produced good fruit, unlike a certain fig tree Jesus passed during his last week in Jerusalem.

Looking for something to eat, Jesus spotted the tree lush with leaves. Since a fig tree produces fruit before sprouting leaves, Jesus walked toward it, expecting figs. Instead, he found the tree without fruit.

Leaves masked its barrenness. Figs should have been there, ripe for picking. Yet, the tree produced nothing. Jesus cursed the tree. Its long life was not good enough (Mark 11:12-14).

At the close of Marcus's memorial service, the pastor asked the question on everyone's mind, "How can I or anyone make sense of such a senseless death? Last night I prayed, 'God, I don't know what to say. What message can his death possibly have for us?'"

The minister scanned his audience. "God answered me, 'March 4th.'"

"March 4th?" he asked, cocking his head and furrowing his brow. "Okay, God, but what message can I deliver? God said, 'Not March 4th. But, March Forth.'"

The minister delivered God's message to us. March forth. Marcus left a legacy of marching forth, growing as a man of God and helping others turn their potential into reality. For those who came to honor his memory, it was now our turn. Our turn to *March Forth* and do the same. March forth because a long life might not be good enough, but a good life is always long enough.

CONNECTING THE DOTS

Each year on March 4, take a moment to assess. While we added another year to life, have we also added life to our years?

Are we playing it safe and living a long life that might or might not be good enough? Or are we living a good life that will always be long enough?

31

For whoever wants to save his life will lose it, but whoever loses his life for me and for the gospel will save it. What good is it for a man to gain the whole world, yet forfeit his soul?
Mark 8:35-36 (NIV)

10

REMEMBER[6]

· · · · · · · · ●● ⬤ ●● · · · · · · ·

We were three pictures away from Grandma's house. Three state lines to pass over before reaching our traditional vacation destination. Three times for Dad to rouse us kids from car games or slumber against the station wagon window.

"We're crossing another state line. Let's get our picture," he announced from the driver's seat.

Our answer was a mix of yawns, snorts, and moans, "Do we have to?"

"Yes, years from now we need to remember where we traveled," he replied. "C'mon!"

We tumbled out of the car. Four kids, Mom, Dad, and our Chihuahua, El Toro.

Dad lined us up. We leaned against the signposts and rolled our eyes as he took the next five minutes to adjust every aperture and setting on his new Canon camera. Then he realigned us under the "Welcome to _____." (Fill in the state, and we have the picture.)

Slides actually. Carefully dated and stacked in sequence in the scratched and dented metal box Dad purchased to store our memories.

I flipped the two latches down, now stiff from years of neglect and disuse. I peeled back the duct tape Dad put on either side of the locks as extra insurance in case the chest fell off the top shelf in his closet.

Inside…our childhood memorialized. Every state line we crossed. Every Easter egg we hunted. I lingered over every house we moved into, Santa we visited, and Christmas gift we opened under our silver tinsel tree.

In one afternoon, a box of slides brought to life memories of the fun our family experienced together despite cramped quarters of fitting two adults and four children into a mid-sized sedan; how we combatted boredom by playing "I Spy" travel games over the long miles; how Dad stopped for us to stretch our legs and for Mom to break out the lunch she prepared to fill our empty bellies. The slides commemorated who we were as a family and how we grew under Dad's watchful eye.

I mumbled a prayer of thanks and apologized to Dad for grousing at every stop to stand by a state welcome sign. I hoped he heard it from his front seat in heaven. His words, now engraved upon my heart and mind, help me recall a faithful father whose love travels with me through every mountain, valley, or prairie I pass. "We need to remember where we traveled, what we did."

CONNECTING THE DOTS

Recall. Reminisce. Remember. Find a way to commemorate passing over "one state line" to another along life's journey. Find a way to keep alive memories of how the Lord "…bore us up on eagles' wings…" (Exodus 19:4, NRSV) and delivered us from our "Egypt."

As God led His Israelite children through the desert, He often repeated one word, "Remember…" Remember escaping slavery in Egypt to cross the Red Sea and later the Jordan River on dry land. Remember victories over enemies and enough daily provision of food and water. Remember the great lengths Father-God went to save and shape them no matter how many times they complained or turned their backs on Him.

That was God with them. That is God with you. That is God with me.

I remember when loneliness smothered me, and a friend crossed my path. I recollect when I didn't have enough, and something happened to provide what I needed; when a situation boxed me in but a pathway through suddenly opened; or when I thought I could not take another step yet found the strength to do so.

Remembering stirs my hope for the future and assurance that God is with me always. It encourages and empowers me to persevere through the next difficult situation. Sometimes, I remember by writing these stories or journaling. Other times, I keep scrapbooks of special moments.

If we do not remember, we can soon forget who God is and what He's done for us. Forgetting leaves space for distrust in His love and faithfulness to move in. Fear follows, along with anxiety, wandering onto dangerous paths, or giving up without a fight.

Mom often said, "Your father loves and lives for you kids. He would do anything for you." And so is the love of the heavenly Father for each of us. Recall. Reminisce. Remember.

> ... *be careful that you do not forget the LORD, who brought you out of Egypt, out of the land of slavery ... it was because the LORD loved you and kept the oath he swore to your ancestors that he brought you out with a mighty hand and redeemed you from the land of slavery ... Know therefore that the LORD your God is God; he is the faithful God, keeping his covenant of love to a thousand generations of those who love him and keep his commandments.*
> Deuteronomy 6:12; 7:8-9 (NIV)

SECTION 2

LIFE'S LIKE THAT

11

THE LESSON OF SUPERMAN

· · · · · · ● ● ● ◉ ● ● ● ● ● ● · · · ·

"Let's play Superman!" Jay,* my next-door neighbor and best playmate, beckoned to me from his front porch. He bounced down the steps followed by his older sister, Rhonda.*

I hesitated. I never liked doing new things that I didn't know how to do right the first time. I watched Superman on television and imagined I was his girlfriend, Lois Lane. But I was not sure how to play Superman because I was a girl, for heaven's sake.

"C'mon," Jay motioned me to come to where he and Rhonda now stood in the middle of their yard. "You'll like it, I promise. Watch."

At Jay's nod, Rhonda sat down on the ground and rolled onto her back, arms spread out from her sides. She brought both her legs up toward her chest. With knees bent and ankles touching, the bottom of Rhonda's feet faced the heavens and formed a "foot stool". Jay stood with his backside to Rhonda. He eased two steps back and propped himself on her "foot stool."

I startled when Jay unexpectedly yelled, "Su - per - man." On cue, Rhonda lowered her legs and shot them skyward with all her might. Jay flew like a pebble out of a slingshot. For about three seconds. He landed with a thump in the carpet-like St. Augustine grass and rolled a few feet before coming to a stop. Jay jumped up laughing hysterically, thrilled by his ride.

"Try it," he coaxed me again.

Should I? I always dreamed of soaring through the sky. What can it hurt? I crossed into Jay's yard. Rhonda got into position and waited for me to sit on her feet. I wobbled, trying to balance. Jay took my hand, helping me to steady, then backed away. I yelled at the top of my lungs, "Su - per - man," and shrieked with laughter as my skinny body heaved toward the heavens.

At the peak of my flight I straightened, overcorrected, and came tumbling back to earth stomach first. The ground came up fast and crumpled my arms beneath me as I hit the grassy landing strip.

Craaaaack. A sharp pain took my breath away as if someone drove a six-inch spike through my right shoulder. I stood and fought back tears while holding my shoulder that drooped inches lower than it did minutes earlier.

After a frantic car ride to the emergency room, the doctor pronounced to my parents what was obvious on the displayed x-ray, "broken collarbone." He turned from them to me, "How'd that happen?"

"I was pretending to be Superman," I wailed.

"Best stick with being Lois Lane in the future," he retorted with a smile.

Maybe so, but how could I know these things unless I pushed my fear aside and at least tried? After all, I soared for a moment. And I knew how to do better next time.

So, I decided that I will stretch beyond my fears again. Why? Because today, even though I wore a cast as a plaster signboard advertising that one miscalculation, I overheard the doctor's parting words to my parents, "Don't worry. She'll heal to fly another day." And sure enough, I did.

CONNECTING THE DOTS

Never fear when God beckons. Step out in faith. Stretch into an unknown, for He promises always to be with us, to give us the power and strength to face any situation.

Words like *do not be afraid* and *fear not* occur over 300 times in the Bible. Inevitably, times come when we find ourselves in new and anxiety-ridden circumstances – either by our choice, the result of someone else's action, or God's calling. When we do, rather than letting fear paralyze us, seek God and His wisdom. He will use trials to stretch and grow us as His beloved child. And if we miss, mess, or miscalculate, don't worry. He heals us to fly another day.

> *So do not fear, for I am with you; do not be dismayed,*
> *for I am your God. I will strengthen you and help you;*
> *I will uphold you with my righteous right hand.*
> Isaiah 41:10 (NIV)

*Not their real names.

41

12

THE VOICE

· · · · · · · · ● · · · · · · · ·

Does God even hear me? Another prayer went unanswered. My cry for help seemed to bounce off the ceiling without reaching through to heaven. Or maybe it fell off the priority ladder when compared to the millions of requests that go His way.

My husband interrupted my musing to remind me it was time to leave. We headed to our only daughter's last choir concert in her senior year at high school.

As proud parents, we rushed to arrive at the auditorium early for a front row seat. Video camera in hand, we were ready to capture every "last" activity in our child's final year before college.

She told us we would see her best by sitting on the right side. We grabbed seats five rows back, right side, as 1,000 other parents, friends, and family of the choir crowded into the auditorium.

The choir of about 125 kids filed on stage and onto the bleachers. We spotted Jessica early. She landed on the second from the top bleacher on the right-hand side as anticipated. The sharp curve of the bleachers and the number of kids in front of her, however, was *not* anticipated. All we could see was her nose and part of the side of her face as she faced left.

I jumped up in frustration, searching for a better spot and view only to find every seat filled except in the distant balcony. Lights dimmed and the choir director walked onto the stage to greet the audience. I had no choice but to plop back in my chair, frustrated at the missed opportunity for a good view or picture of our daughter's final concert.

The 125 students began their first song. With arms folded and eyes squeezed shut, I took deep breaths to calm my disappointment.

That's when I heard it. That voice.

The same voice that ran the scales and practiced this song in our dining room for the last six weeks. The same voice that chattered about her day over the dinner table. The same voice that shared her hurts and dreams while she and I crowded into a tiny bathroom to get ready every morning. Jessica's voice. The strains of her mezzo soprano fell on my ears, clear and distinct from the other 124 around her. That voice penetrated through the crowd of sopranos, altos, basses, and baritones all singing at once. Because I knew my daughter so well, I knew her voice.

Then I knew. God knows me. He hears me, too.

CONNECTING THE DOTS

Surely, if I, a mere mortal, can distinguish the voice of my child, who I know so well and love so dearly, then our Almighty God-Father and Creator can distinguish the voice of each of His children, too.

God knows us, and He knows our voice. He can distinguish our every praise and cry for help. Even when we don't think He's listening, He is.

As for me, I call to God, and the LORD saves me. Evening,
morning and noon I cry out in distress, and he hears my voice.
Psalm 55:16-17 (NIV)

13

HOW LONG IS TEMPORARY?

· · · · · · · · · ● · · · · · · · · · ·

The curve on the sign at the end of Loop 288 warned drivers. As they zipped along the highway at posted 60 mph speed limits, the hairpin turn forced them to almost stop in order to navigate the road that led to Interstate 35W. Below the picture in bold black letters was one word, *temporary.*

I first spotted this sign seven, going on eight, years earlier when returning home from visiting our daughter in her home in Aubrey, Texas. Then, when my husband and I moved to this area, I saw it every day on my route to work.

The problem is that I measure *temporary* in terms of hours or days, maybe weeks at the outside. Not years or decades. But here, I saw no indication *temporary* would change any time soon.

A few weeks ago, and ten years since my first trip through this section of highway, I traveled the route again to attend a meeting. Sure enough, the only change was the road sign. Instead of *Temporary*, it now said *Detour* with a picture of the same hairpin turn below.

CONNECTING THE DOTS

Expect hairpin turns. Some are temporary. Some are permanent detours.

Life's like that. Inevitably something unexpected interrupts our path, and we enter a hairpin turn of circumstances. Illness, betrayal, job loss, loneliness, loss of a dream, a broken relationship, or some other painful experience. Something we did not ask for.

Likewise, temporary turns can last longer than we expect or want. We hope for brief, short-lived. Yet, as temporary drags on without an end in sight, fear of permanent can set in. Anxiety may strangle us when we don't know or see how we are going to survive through it.

When life throws in a hairpin turn, I discovered the best way to manage it is to slow down and trust God to carry me through on His promises.

As a young man, God promised David a kingship. However, David then spent seventeen years in a detour, running from his enemy and hiding in caves before he finally rose to the throne. Moses led the Israelites out of Egypt and slavery toward the Promised Land and freedom. Yet, they encountered a 40-year detour before crossing the Jordan River into their destination. The prophet Isaiah foretold of a king who would restore the people to their land, yet they were persecuted and scattered like pollen in the wind before the Savior, Jesus Christ, redeemed them some 400 years later.

How did they manage detours? They trusted in a promise…God's promise that He never leaves us nor forsakes us while He connects the dots in our story. The promise that *temporary*, no matter how long term, is not the permanent end in His hands. Our hope is in Christ. We can trust that He will light the way through those hairpin turns until our feet rest again on a firm foundation and our path is made straight.

In his kindness, God called you to share in his eternal
glory by means of Christ Jesus. So after you have suffered
a little while, he will restore, support, and strengthen
you, and he will place you on a firm foundation.
1 Peter 5:10 (NLT)

14

THE ANNOYING IMPORTANCE OF PATIENCE

• • • • • • • • • ● • • • • • • • • •

Not one to wait patiently, I looked for the quickest way to vary my exercise routine, strengthen the core without crunches, and achieve instant toning. My answer came from a childhood pastime — the hula hoop.

I was an adept hula hooping ten-year-old, able to keep three at a time twirling my waist for over a hundred reps before they fell in a tangled heap. So, I sent my husband in search of the perfect hula hoop. He brought home a sky blue one adorned with flashers. I envisioned instant success.

I cleared a space, poised the hoop at my waist and shoved it into a whirl. Clack! Two reps later, its flashers sparkled on the floor. I tried again...and again. After fifteen minutes and gasping from exertion, I maxed out at six hulas before losing the hoop to my feet. So much for instant success.

Reality set in. I wasn't ten years old anymore. My goal of re-conquering the hula hoop would come, but only after a time with patience, practice, and perseverance.

CONNECTING THE DOTS

Saying "yes" to God's calls or assignments in life often requires patience, practice, and perseverance. Success rarely comes instantly. Annoying as that reality may be, we usually gain ground and progress a little at a time toward bigger visions, higher goals, or deeper passions.

Jesus told a parable of a poor and powerless widow who nagged a corrupt and compassionless judge for justice against her opponent. At first, the judge refused. The widow persisted with dogged determination. Her staying power finally wore the judge down, and he granted her the justice she sought (Luke 18:1-8).

God's not making something happen at once doesn't mean He isn't working on it with us and for us. Blessings come when we tenaciously press forward in our course of action; if we patiently endure to obey the Lord; if we stay in the game despite its stress and strain.

Case in point — three days later, I was up to 30 hula revolutions.

*Blessed is the one who perseveres under trial because,
having stood the test, that person will receive the crown of
life that the Lord has promised to those who love him.*
James 1:12 (NIV)

15

EASIEST WAY TO
CHOKE OUT WEEDS

· · · · · · ● ● ● ● ● ◉ ● ● ● ● ● ● · · · · ·

"Give it up," Jim suggested in the middle of my back-breaking, muscle straining weed pulling. "You can't beat weeds that way. We'll fertilize and healthy grass will choke 'em out."

"You're just being lazy and don't want to help me." Sarcasm and sweat dripped off my brow as I uprooted another intruder.

After Jim disappeared into the garage, the next door neighbor chased his two-year old down the sidewalk to where I squatted and dug in the dirt.

"Weeds, huh?" he commented. "We had that problem, too, when we first moved in. We just fertilized and let the grass choke them out." I peered around the neighbor's two-year old and envied his weed-less lawn.

"Yeah, I heard that somewhere."

Five buckets of Johnson grass and henbit later, I broke for lunch. Wanting to justify my time and effort, I grabbed my gardening bible, *Neil Sperry's Complete Guide to Texas Gardening*. The lawn prophet wrote, *Even the best lawns have weeds. They're as inevitable in Texas landscapes and gardens as dry soil and bugs.*[1]

Well then, how, pray tell, does one get rid of those obnoxious plants?

Sperry's answer, *For starters, don't pull them. The best weed killers of all may be a bag of lawn fertilizer and a functioning lawn sprinkler. Vigorous turf discourages weeds.*[2] Translation ... healthy grass chokes out weeds. Dang, pride just cost me hours of sweaty labor for naught.

Weeds are inevitable. They spring up everywhere without anyone planting them. Without a healthy lawn, pulling them does not help. They grow right back. Instead, the best antidote: fertilizer and water to nurture healthy grass that grows so thick that it chokes out the weeds.

CONNECTING THE DOTS

Experience taught me that spiritual weeds are inevitable as well. They, too, can spring up easily. Weeds, whose roots lie within my human, self-centered heart. Weeds like pride, prejudice, fear, and selfishness. If left untended or overlooked, spiritual weeds spread rapidly, only to leave my spiritual life growing thin and bare of the good works for which God created me.

The best antidote: Choke out spiritual weeds by feeding our souls daily with a healthy dose of God's Word and a drenching with the living water that only Jesus Christ gives. Let His Holy Spirit take root and grow dense within every nook and cranny of our being. The result yields a bountiful, healthy harvest of good fruit – love, joy, peace, patience, kindness, generosity, faithfulness, gentleness, and self-control (Galatians 5:22).

Get rid of all moral filth and the evil that is so prevalent and humbly accept the word implanted in you, which can save you.
James 1:21 (NIV)

16

A STITCH IN TIME

· · · · · · ● ● ● ● ● ● ● ● · · · · ·

It began as a failed guitar lesson. "You'll make a better quilter than guitar picker," Mama Walker said after an unsuccessful lesson in guiding my six year-old fingers across wire strings and frets on her guitar. "C'mon. I'll show you how."

My grandmother, mom's mother, led me to a corner of the middle room in her East Dallas shotgun-styled home. On a chair lay a pile of scrap fabrics — a mix of florals, geometrics, stripes and calicoes.

"Pick what you like," she waved her hand toward the material. For the next two hours, I cut 3"x3" squares using the cardboard pattern Mama Walker fashioned from the cover of a steno pad.

"You're done with the first step," she commented while peering over my shoulder. "Time to stitch blocks together. I'll show you how."

Mama Walker motioned me to the chair in front of her trestle sewing machine. The machine from which she magically created aprons, bonnets, dresses, and quilts. "This way," she instructed. "Solids against prints. Three to a row. Three rows to make a nine-square block. Here, you can do it."

I plopped in the chair and pumped the peddle. The machine whirred to life. My confidence grew with each rise and fall of the needle to the rhythm of my foot.

"Slow down. Don't hurry," Mama Walker cautioned when my foot speed increased, and the needle ate fabric faster than I could match seams. By dinner time I stacked enough squares to cover my twin bed at home.

Over the next month and with hands gnarled by arthritis, Mama Walker pieced my fabric blocks together, quilted the top, and finished the raw edges.

Years later, I fingered the now-worn quilt retrieved from the bottom of my quilt box. Close up, I noticed the non-squared squares and uneven stitches from my six year-old effort. I eyed telltale holes where I ripped apart seams after discovering a right side sewn to a wrong side of fabric. I spied traces of knotted thread where my erratic foot rhythm on the trestle tensed the spool of twine feeding the needle.

Yet, when I looked at the quilt from across the room, mistakes vanished. A shabby chic twin bed topper remained, its beauty in its wholistic vintage look. Its perfection lay in its not-so-perfectly assembled pattern.

And I smile in awe of Mama Walker. How patiently she guided my hands and helped me course-correct mistakes. How she took my misshapen squares and stitched them together to fashion them into something useful and of vintage beauty.

CONNECTING THE DOTS

Even when my attempts to do or create deliver less than perfect results, the Lord finds a way to use them. He recalls, repairs, and redeploys my misses and messes to stitch them together for my good or that of others.

Jesus did the same with his disciple, Peter. Always the impulsive one, Peter swore He would follow Jesus even if it led to death. After soldiers arrested Jesus, that same Peter denied His Lord three times. Realizing his mistake and crushed by shame, he returned to life as a fisherman. But the resurrected Jesus sought him out.

> He recalls, repairs, and redeploys our misses and messes to stitch them together for our good or that of others.

Over breakfast on the shores of Galilee, the Lord pulled Peter aside. He took Peter's mess, forgave him, and then re-called, restored, and reaffirmed Peter's purpose – to build His church and feed people with the good news of a risen Christ (John 21:1-17).

Where we see mess, the Lord sees merit. If we let Him, He transforms our life's knotted threads, mismatched seams, and shortcomings into a quilt of beauty, stitched together to serve *His* purposes.

He has made everything beautiful in its time.
Ecclesiastes 3:11 (NIV)

17

UNTYING THE KNOTS

• • • • • • • • ● • • • • • • • • •

Living through Lent and the corona virus pandemic in 2020 gave me time to reflect on the state of my heart. As days of social distancing and isolation lumbered into weeks four and five, I sometimes found my thoughts twisted into knots of negativity and self-centered focus.

What I did *not* have, could *not* do, or may *not* be able to fulfill in the future, all crowded my mind. Thoughts that consequently fueled my heart with periodic boredom, anxiety, loneliness, and discontent. These, in turn, spiraled into my age-old enemy – a giant knotted feeling of inadequacy.

Thoughts (in our mind) drive feelings (in our heart). Feelings drive behavior (in our actions). Consequently, the makings of my pity-party were in the works.

The greatest enemy to my contentment and well-being was within me. What I needed was to work on changing how I was thinking, to stop the negative "nots."

I ran across a prayer I saved from a church newsletter eight Lenten seasons ago. Instead of letting negative thoughts take over my heart, The Knot Prayer reminded me to work on rooting them out and change the way I thought about circumstances and myself. It gave me a start to battle the enemies of my heart…

Dear God,

Please untie the knots in my mind, my heart and my life.

Remove the have nots, the can nots, and the do nots that I have in my mind.

Erase the will nots, may nots, might nots that may find a home in my heart.

Release me from the could nots, would nots and should nots that obstruct my life.

And most of all, dear God, I ask that you remove from my mind, my heart and my life all of the "am nots" that I have allowed to hold me back, especially the thought that I am not good enough. Amen[3]

CONNECTING THE DOTS

We must recognize and battle the enemies within. These "nots" are the root causes of negative feelings and behaviors that separate us from the Lord and others.

We discover and can live God's promised abundant life when we first untie the "nots" in our thoughts, which will, in turn, untie knots of fear in our stomach. Then, replace those "nots" instead with those greater things – with the "is-es" listed by the Apostle Paul:

Finally, brothers and sisters, whatever is true, whatever is noble, whatever is right, whatever is pure, whatever is lovely, whatever is admirable-if anything is excellent or praiseworthy-think about such things…and the God of peace will be with you.
Philippians 4:8-9 (NIV)

18

ASK, BEFORE IT'S TOO LATE

· · · · · · ● ● ● ● ⬤ ● ● ● ● ● ● · · ·

After Daddy died, I still grieved nine months later. I ached for one last hug and yearned to know the answer to my biggest question. Was he in heaven?

My father's genial manner attracted friendships, but he never spoke about his faith. Worse yet, I never asked. Church attendance served him as a social event, but did it draw him closer to God?

In the weeks after Daddy died, I discovered possible evidence of his faith journey…the *Promise Keepers* book left on his bedside table, the *Incomparable Jesus Bible Study* stacked in a magazine rack, and the pastor's stories of Daddy's involvement in adult Sunday school. Even my husband dreamed about Daddy saying, "Don't worry, I'm in a good place."

Still, I harbored doubts. I wanted an indisputable sign. None came.

Doubts and grief weighed on me heavier than usual one morning, like I was swimming a mile-wide lake, fully dressed in a wool coat and boots. To console my aching heart, I donned a pair of Daddy's favorite cufflinks. Blue-grey stones mounted on silver, they always stood in sharp contrast against his starched, white shirts as he headed for his office.

While driving to work, I popped in a CD. The toe-tapping, finger-snapping gospel sang about an individual's joy in walking along the highway to heaven. I smiled at the lyrics, when… mid-chorus, and while stopped at a red light, my eye caught movement on the shoulder of the road. I glanced over and spotted him — Daddy. Walking along the highway, surrounded by a crowd, laughing and talking.

He turned toward me, smiled and waved. His words weren't audible, but my heart heard him say, "I'm on the highway to heaven, honey!"

Then, he rejoined his companions, and I lost sight of him. I strained to will his image back. Was it really Daddy? Or just power of suggestion for what I wanted to be real?

Honking horns jerked my attention back to the now green light. I pulled forward reluctantly, checking my rearview mirror, desperately wanting to catch one last glimpse of my father. The sidewalk was empty.

Later that morning, as I left an operations briefing, I absent-mindedly fingered Daddy's cufflink on by blouse. Then panicked. The stone was missing. Somewhere between home and that meeting, the stone fell off the left cufflink. But, where?

I frantically searched my office. Nothing.

I retraced my steps twice through aisles of associate cubicles where I walked earlier and from parking garage to department. Still no stone. Losing it again ripped open the wound of losing him.

"Please, God," I prayed. "Let me find it. The stone has no value. Let me keep Daddy's memory whole."

In a last-ditch effort, I slowly snaked my way again up and down rows of cubicles. Near the end of the last aisle, I spotted it against the blue, multi-colored carpet. A corner of the blue-grey, dime-sized stone peaked out from under an associate's desk.

Bending to retrieve my treasure, I rejoiced and silently praised God. Only He could give me Superman-like vision to distinguish something so tiny, well hidden, and blending into a similar-colored carpet. Only His grace kept it from being missed and swept away by night cleaning crews.

CONNECTING THE DOTS

Pray God opens doors of opportunity to engage family, friends, neighbors, and anyone He places in our path, in intentional faith conversations. Then, before it is too late, walk through that door.

My celebration over recovered treasure re-connected me to a similar story. Jesus told a parable about a woman who lost a valuable coin. After a desperate search, she found it and celebrated with a party.

God sent me in search of this parable. I was too late for a faith conversation with Dad to assure me of his salvation. Yet, God's grace washed away my doubts. The parable's closing words caught my breath as Jesus explained the message:

In the same way, I tell you, there is rejoicing in the presence of the angels of God over one sinner who repents.
Luke 15:10 (NIV)

Two God-given signs pointed me to truth about Dad. The cufflink lost and found. And the thin veil between heaven and earth that dropped momentarily to let me see Daddy walking the highway to heaven. My father was saved. I rejoiced. God and the angels rejoiced.

19

WHEN TURNING BACK
MOVES YOU FORWARD

· · · · · · · · ● · · · · · · · · ·

With windshield wipers flapping against a light drizzle, I waved goodbye to my sister, standing on the front porch of her home nestled in the woods of East Texas. We spent the afternoon catching up on our lives. I had stopped by on my way to a nearby retreat center where I would lead a corporate planning event.

"The retreat center is only a few miles down this road," her husband assured me. "A sign marks the path leading to the place."

Clutching directions, I reassured myself with famous last words, "Easy schmeasy. Out of the driveway turn right. The retreat center is only a hop, skip, and a jump away."

Drizzle suddenly became driving rain that pounded my windshield, and the dusky sky turned pitch black. I forgot ... no streetlights in the country. Turning the wipers up a notch and slowing the car, I strained to catch sight of the lodge's sign. Nothing.

I reached a dead end where my brother-in-law's words echoed in my brain, "If you reach a dead end, you've gone too far." I turned around and retraced my steps. Back and forth on the one-lane country road I went — three times.

As time neared to kick off the planning meeting, I was not too proud to ask for directions. A house set far back off the road with lights on looked promising. In the dark and halfway up their driveway, I realized it wasn't paved. Too late. Wheels bogged down in the muddy mess and spun in place.

Tears welled, and I choked back a sob, "God, please help me." I rocked the car back and forth for what seemed an eternity. Finally, traction.

Turning around, I headed back toward the road and my sister's house. I needed someone who knew these darkened, country lanes to guide me. Her husband offered, "Follow me. I'll signal you where to turn."

Less than five minutes later, his right turn signal flashed. Slowing my speed to a crawl, the narrow, unlit road to the retreat center came into view of my headlights. A wooden sign not more than 18" x 4" in size and a foot off the ground pointed the way. I honked a thank-you and breathed a sigh of relief. I was back on the right path.

CONNECTING THE DOTS

When we discover we're charging down the wrong way:

Turn around. That's what John the Baptist and the prophets meant when they called God's people to *repent.* When lost or headed in the wrong direction, we must turn around and go back in order to find the right way forward again.

Re-establish traction forward. While searching our way out of darkness, we may find ourselves mired in ruts of habits that threaten forward progress. Spinning our wheels in that place only digs us in a deeper hole. Instead, break the old habit and begin a new one that re-establishes traction and forward momentum in the right direction.

Don't go it alone. Our power, knowledge, and experience are never enough. When lost, back up and turn toward the One who always waits and willingly shows us the right road. The One who says, "Follow me. Turn here."

Manasseh, Judah's fourteenth and perhaps most wicked king, learned these lessons all too well. Committed to idolatry, he seduced Judah to evil ways. Only after defeated and deported to Babylonia did he repent and move the Israelites forward once more.

But while in deep distress, Manasseh sought the Lord his God and sincerely humbled himself before the God of his ancestors. And when he prayed, the Lord listened to him and was moved by his request. So, the Lord brought Manasseh back to Jerusalem and to his kingdom. Then Manasseh finally realized that the Lord alone is God!
2 Chronicles 33:12-13 (NLT)

20

SMILE, BE OF GOOD CHEER

· · · · · · · · ● ● ● · · · · · · · · · ·

I met the couple in the hospital's lobby where I worked. As social work director, I toured families in quest of the best physical rehabilitation center to treat their loved one after a traumatic event. Some looked for miracles following paralyzing spinal cord injuries; others sought help in the aftermath of head injuries or strokes. Yet, one common thread linked the families. They all searched for hope.

> A smile ... can console the inconsolable; encourage the discouraged; erase fear from the fearful; and restore hope to the hopeless.

This particular mother and father's eighteen-year-old daughter sustained a life-changing head injury in a car accident. Two weeks later, stable and awake from a coma, doctors suggested she enter physical rehab.

"You're our third and final facility to visit," Mom offered. Her voice trembled slightly. That and her moist eyes gave away her effort not to cry. Dad's curt nod and darting glances everywhere around the lobby betrayed his own struggle to keep feelings in check.

As Mom described their search, I recognized the competition — a hospital who recently re-opened their doors in a spacious, state-of-the-art building and a rehab center well-known for its treatment of head injuries. Wondering how our modest, three-year-old facility would stack up against these powerhouses, I began the parents' tour.

We arrived back in the lobby forty-five minutes later, after observing therapy sessions and greeting physical therapists, doctors, and nurses. Without preamble, Mom turned to me and said, "We've decided you're the right facility for our daughter."

"Wonderful," I blinked, surprised at such a quick decision. "What differentiated us?"

"That's easy," Mom replied. Her eyes watered. "I counted the smiles. On the faces of your patients and your staff. You win."

"Smiles?" I didn't grasp her logic.

Tears spilled onto Mom's cheeks. "Yes, smiles. They give us hope."

Connecting the Dots

Smile. Be of good cheer wherever you can, as often as you can.

A smile takes small effort but can make a big difference. It can console the inconsolable; encourage the discouraged; erase fear from the fearful; and restore hope to the hopeless.

Two thousand years ago, God sent us His Son, Jesus Christ. Through him, our Creator radiated His light, smiling through the darkness to give us hope for victory over evil and death.

These things I have spoken to you, that in Me you may have peace. In the world you will have tribulation; but be of good cheer, I have overcome the world.
John 16:33 (NKJV)

SECTION 3

SOMEBODY SHOULD'VE SAID SOMETHING

21

THE MISSING INGREDIENT[1]

· · · · · · · · · ●●●◉●●●● · · · · · · · ·

My dinner guests arrived right on time, but not me. I dizzily darted about the kitchen running late. Still needing to fix the cornbread, I greeted my friends, served hors d'oeuvres, and excused myself to finish preparations.

Because Mom did not pass along her creative cooking gene, I followed the recipe to the letter. *Cornmeal – check. Eggs – got 'em. Milk – double check. Baking powder … where's my baking powder? Dang, I don't have any. Oh, well, it's only ¼ teaspoon. I'll just skip it.*

I mixed, stirred, poured and popped the pan into the oven. Twenty minutes later I pulled out a sizzling, golden brown, quarter-inch deep cornbread "hockey puck." How could one ingredient, like baking powder, in so tiny of an amount, make such a huge difference?

That's the same question I often asked myself in life. How could my ¼ teaspoon of whatever be enough to make much difference? As a result, I often resisted or declined stepping forward whenever I assessed myself as lacking – when I did not count myself as schooled, experienced, positioned, statured, or developed enough to meet the demands of a situation or opportunity.

So, I'll skip it, I thought. *Who will notice or miss me? Surely, someone better will step up.* More often than not, I saw myself as too little to make a difference. Only after regrets of missed opportunities and with encouragement from mentors, did I realize my little ¼ teaspoon *can* make a difference.

CONNECTING THE DOTS

God values each of us. We each have a part He wants us to play in His plan for creation.

Where we hear God's call, we can trust He wants us specifically – not someone else – to jump into the mix. Even when one part stands out more prominently than others, each plays an important role for the best result. No one ingredient is the whole recipe for whatever God is creating at the time. And no unnecessary part exists. Whether we are His one cup of cornmeal, or His two eggs, or His ¼ teaspoon of baking powder, each part matters.

We must never underestimate our ¼ teaspoon. Until we get into it, who knows how that too-small-to-count ¼ teaspoon counts in the mix? It may serve as the catalyst that causes the whole thing to rise.

From him the whole body, joined and held together
by every supporting ligament, grows and builds
itself up in love, as each part does its work.
Ephesians 4:16 (NIV)

22

THE HEART'S DESIRE

· · · · · · · · · ● · · · · · · · · ·

The manager closed my office door. He came to talk out a troubling situation with one of his direct reports.

When the young man interviewed, he boasted of being a Great White in the ocean of sales. Yet, his results were those of a sardine. A bottom dweller in stack ranks. Despite the plastic shark he placed on his desk as a reminder of his promise, he was not a sales shark at heart.

After reviewing the month's results, the manager leaned back in his chair and studied the young man sitting across from him. Eyes downcast, shoulders drooped, sweaty hands gripped knees.

"Short of targets again, huh?" the young man said. He drew in a long breath, and confessed, "I don't think this job is a good fit for me."

"So, where *is* your heart?" the manager asked. "If you could do anything with your life, what would you do?"

"I'd be a nurse."

Of all possible answers, the manager never fathomed that response from someone working in sales in finance. Somewhere, amidst the young man's story peppered with ought-to's and have-to's, he dashed desires of his heart against am-nots and can-nots. He gave up against obstacles he couldn't see how to overcome. He got hung up on sandbars of doubt and fear. And, he now risked wallowing in self-pity for failing to live up to expectations.

"So, what do you want to do?" I prodded the manager after hearing the story. His answer was that of a true leader who looked beyond the immediate problem and easy answers.

Rather than issue a performance warning, the manager called the associate back to his dream. He bargained to coach him toward satisfactory performance in his current position while at the same time helping him find a path to nursing. Three years later the young man resigned to enter nursing school. Today, he's an RN, living out his true purpose, his heart's desire.

CONNECTING THE DOTS

Discover someone's heart's desire and help them get there.

The apostle Peter, too, failed to live up to expectations. He denied Christ three times. Guilt-ridden, Peter returned to his former life as a fisherman. Perhaps he thought that was all he was meant for after failure to live up to his promise to follow Christ to prison and death (John 21:1-17).

Yet, Jesus surprised Peter. The risen Christ came looking for his disciple. From the seashore, Jesus called to Peter and his companions, "Friends...." And He called Peter back to his heart's desire ... to be the rock. Not the rock on which dreams were dashed, but the rock on which Christ built his church.

...for it is God who works in you to will and to
act according to his good purpose.
Philippians 2:13 (NIV)

23

UP FROM THE GRAVE: PART 1
MIRACLES HAPPEN

· · · · · · · · ● ◉ ● · · · · · · · · ·

Eleanor struggled against the onslaught of cancer. Diagnosed six months earlier with multiple myeloma, she entered the hospital with severe pain and advancing disease.

I sat in the nurse's station while the oncologist reviewed Eleanor's chart. I was the social worker assigned to the hospital's cancer unit. "Her counts don't look good," he said, flipping through pages of nursing notes and lab work. "She's not responding to treatment this time."

"And we can't wake her up," the head nurse added as she joined us for morning rounds.

Dr. W tossed the chart aside and stood. "Well, let's go see her." The head nurse and I followed him down the hallway to Eleanor's room.

Inside, a breakfast tray rested untouched on the stand beside Eleanor. An intravenous pole at the head of her bed held a plastic bag half full of glucose. The solution slowly dripped into tiny tubing that threaded its way to her arm. Eleanor's petite body lay motionless beneath the sheet and mauve pink blanket.

"Eleanor, can you wake up for me?" Dr W tapped her arm with the back of his hand. "Open your eyes, Eleanor, breakfast is here." She didn't move. He shook her shoulder gently. Her eyes remained closed. Only the sheet rose and fell as Eleanor breathed in short, shallow gulps.

Bending over her, Dr. W pressed his stethoscope against her chest. "Slow heart rate, too. I doubt she'll last through the evening." Even I recognized the signs. Eleanor's life ebbed away.

We pushed on to see other patients, but I couldn't shake the boulder of sorrow that crushed my objective social worker resolve. Eleanor was one of my first patients when I started fresh out of graduate school and full of energy to make a difference. To make things right with the world. But Eleanor's condition was something neither the doctor nor I could make right.

And who would the head nurse notify? I never saw anyone visit Eleanor. I vaguely recalled her telling me about an only daughter. Yet, their relationship lay in rubble, blasted apart by a long-forgotten disagreement. Did the daughter even know her mother was in the hospital?

The next morning the head nurse met the physician and me in the hallway, "You gotta go by Eleanor's room. You're not gonna believe *this*."

We didn't. There sat Eleanor – upright, alert, and enjoying breakfast. Finishing a bite of toast, she smiled and welcomed the entourage to her bedside with a cheerful, "Good morning."

"Well, good morning to you," the oncologist said. He examined Eleanor, pronounced her heart strong and her blood work in good order. She declared her bone pain diminished. "If you keep this up, you can go home by the end of the week."

Dr W shook his head in disbelief as we left the room. In the hallway, out of earshot of Eleanor, he shrugged and speculated, "Maybe the chemo finally kicked in to do their job."

Overnight? When her body was so close to shutting down? "But she was on death's door, right?" I asked the doctor. "Have you ever witnessed such a recovery?"

"No, but it can happen. Not usually, though."

Maybe chemotherapy helped. But I believed this medical miracle signaled God's presence breaking into the oncology unit. He was the only One powerful enough to bring Eleanor back from the brink of death.

I left work soul-satisfied with the ending to Eleanor's story. Yet, that end was only the start of the true stakes in her healing. While we celebrated Eleanor's physical recovery, another miracle quietly unfolded.

CONNECTING THE DOTS

God's Word leaves us with plenty of testimonies where He breaks through and into the natural course of events to heal. Like King Hezekiah who invoked God's compassion to raise him from his deathbed (Isaiah 38:1-8); or Jesus raising Lazarus from the dead after three days in the tomb (Luke 7:11-17). Or like any of the blind, sick, and disabled who experienced God's incredible power through Jesus' healing touch.

God can heal the sick and disabled today as He did in Old and New Testament times. He has the power to overcome His laws of nature and science, or to work through them to produce the incredible. And to give us a taste of the future when all healing will be complete.

Miracles by God do happen.

O Lord my God, I called to you for help and you healed me.
O Lord, you brought me up from the grave;
you spared me from going down into the pit...
weeping may remain for a night,
but rejoicing comes in the morning.
Psalm 30:2-3, 5 (NIV)

24

UP FROM THE GRAVE: PART 2 FROM HURTING TO HEALING

· · · · · · · · · ● · · · · · · · · · ·

After the cancer retreated, Eleanor left the hospital. The multiple myeloma stayed in check for a year before she returned to the oncology unit, out of remission, and suffering with advanced disease. This time, though, Eleanor's creased brow and gritted teeth gave way to a peace absent during earlier admissions. Only laugh lines wrinkled her face around her eyes and Mona Lisa smile.

"Eleanor, tell me how you're feeling." I coaxed her to talk, unable to fathom the change in her demeanor despite recurring cancer and excruciating bone pain. She patted a spot on the bed, motioning me to sit while she reflected on the last time she entered the hospital and lingered near death.

"My daughter said I was in a coma," she said, her voice trembling with weakness. "That's when I saw it. A blinding white light just like they say. I know it was Jesus. I wanted to go with him, but he pointed behind me and said I had to go back. I wasn't done here yet. When I turned around, I saw my daughter enter the room. I wanted to stay with Jesus but couldn't.

"My daughter stood beside me when I opened my eyes. We had rarely spoken for years. Some disagreement or other."

Eleanor paused to catch her breath, now coming in shallow gulps of air. "I was too weak to manage alone at home. You remember. My daughter volunteered to move in with me. I didn't want to disrupt her life but had little choice. So, I agreed."

Eleanor's eyes watered. "She took such good care of me, doing everything. The housework, cooking, taking me to the doctor. She wouldn't let me do anything."

Wincing with pain and drawing in a re-energizing breath, Eleanor continued. "Over the months, my daughter and I talked. Not so much at first. Then a lot. She forgave me."

Eleanor and her daughter had reunited. Through the circumstances of a physical need, mother and daughter opened their hearts to God's grace and healing. The Holy Spirit helped them knit their broken relationship back together.

Three days later, Eleanor died. Peacefully. Her daughter at her side and both giving thanks for the transformational healing received from a compassionate God.

CONNECTING THE DOTS

God uses and can work interruptions, hardships, or unwanted turns in life for our good. He may even have put us or allowed us to come to that moment for reasons we do not initially understand.

Eleanor and her daughter are good examples. God weaved a plan and process for their good. He carried Eleanor from a cancer diagnosis to an eventual need for help in daily activities to her daughter moving in with her. God gave Eleanor a momentary reprieve from physical death to pave the way for another reprieve — that of separation from her child.

We may not initially see or understand God's means of work. Take care not to force a quick solution. Instead, seize the opportunity to grow in faith.

...in all things God works for the good of those who love
him, who have been called according to his purpose.
Romans 8:28 (NIV)

25

THE REAL USE FOR
A COMFORTER

· · · · · · · · ● ● ● ● ● ● ● · · · · · · ·

"What do you think you're doing?!" The wife demanded an answer from her husband of six months. The one wrapped in the couple's new $700 comforter as he lazed on the bed, feet propped, drink in hand, watching a football game.

Startled and confused by her intrusion in his man-cave moment, he hit the mute button. "I don't know. What? What am I doing?"

His wife yanked the comforter off his reclining body and pronounced, "This is for decoration, not to use!" She smoothed the tangled mess and folded it over the end of the bed.

Searching for words of wisdom from those more tenured in marriage, the young husband now shared his story over dinner with our leadership team. Men around the table guffawed in a *yes-we've-all-been-there* tone. The women, including me, stared at him with a *you-should-know-better* look.

"Some things are only for decoration, not use," chided women. "Can't you carry that notion too far?" rebutted our practical male counterparts. Thus went the debate, each person entrenched in defending their perspective.

On the trip home, the question clawed its way back to the surface of my mind. Can we miss the full joy of a gift because we don't use it for its intended purpose? My thoughts shifted into a spiritual gear.

Christ sent to us the Holy Spirit after He paid the high price of dying on the cross. The Spirit's purpose was to comfort us. To counsel, help, encourage, intercede, and advocate in our behalf.

However, I admit that my first-born, I-can-do-it-myself, attitude often led me to hold the Comforter at a distance, as a decoration in my life rather than something to use. Until one day circumstances forced me to admit, "This I cannot do alone." I hadn't heard much about the Holy Spirit from the pulpit. But, on that day I reached out to and wrapped myself in the Comforter. He lifted the yoke of grief from my shoulders.

Frequently on Sundays now, that newlywed's comforter comes to mind in church when prayer blankets are passed from person to person. Each reads the name for whom the blanket is intended, lifts the individual in prayer, and ties a knot in the fringe.

Someone delivers the blanket to the one named on the card. So, when pain, despair, or fear threaten to swamp the one in need, s/he wraps themselves in the blanket. They experience the Comforter, God's Holy Spirit, there for them, walking with them, doing for them what they cannot do alone. These blankets are not just decoration to admire. They are to use.

CONNECTING THE DOTS

Get to know the Holy Spirit, the third person of the Trinity. We can read about Him in numerous scriptures. Several excellent books also exist.[2]

Bottom line: The Holy Spirit is a gift from God who provides us with power for living, understanding spiritual truth, and guidance in doing what is right in the eyes of the Lord. He comes into our hearts the moment we accept Christ as our Savior.

Jesus called the Holy Spirit our Comforter. He was sent by the Father to dwell within us and be available daily for helping, encouraging, interceding, and advocating for us. Like prayer blankets and bed comforters, we can call upon, recline upon, and wrap ourselves in this Comforter every moment of every day. Don't squander or miss out on the full joy of this gift from God.

As Jesus prepared to leave His disciples, He said,

And I will pray to the Father, and he shall give you another Comforter, that he may abide with you forever.
John 14:16 (KJV)

26

ENCOUNTER WITH
THE ENEMY

· · · · · · · · · · ● · · · · · · · · · · ·

The enemy came under cover of darkness.

The snake wound its way up the trunk of the ficus tree, slid into the baby cardinals' nest, and killed them. No noise warned me of what was coming. No ruckus drew me to look on the patio and prevent the attack.

Only when I peeked through the kitchen window for a last glance at the babies before I headed off to bed, did I discover the scaled reptile wrapped around the nest. They hatched four days earlier and now were gone.

Jim's words haunted me. "I'm going to get rid of that, so the bird won't build there," he said when the nest first took shape.

"No," I protested. "Leave the mother alone." The cardinal fascinated me, building a home twig by twig. I "ooohed" and "aaaahed" at the four blue-white eggs resting inside, no bigger than my finger joint. I marveled as mom stood on the nest's edge and dropped bits of food into four outstretched open beaks.

But, too late I realized Jim was right. "Birds build nests in our front yard tree, Gloria, but twenty to thirty feet higher than your ficus. Where nothing can reach them."

I should have listened and stopped the nest-building when Jim suggested it. Blinded by my desire to house a mother cardinal and her babies on my patio, I didn't see the danger. How could something so innocent be so wrong?

CONNECTING THE DOTS

The enemy does exist and takes advantage of any opportunity to steal, kill, and destroy our relationship with God (John 10:10). He slithers in under cover of darkness. His two greatest weapons are temptation and deception.

God's chosen people fell victim to the enemy's deception. They wanted to look and organize like surrounding nations by allowing a king to rule and guide them. Where was the harm (1 Samuel 8)?

The prophet and priest, Samuel, warned the Israelites. They did not need an earthly king to tell them what to do. God was their true king and they were His treasured people who He loved. But the Israelites refused to listen. Nothing but trouble followed with a string of kings who led the people astray and into captivity.

So, I learned a hard lesson. Selfish desire can deceive and cause harm to others as well as myself. It seduces me into thinking something is okay when it is not. That something bad is good or that something dangerous is safe. It blinds and deludes me into imagining I control the situation or outcome.

I will now remember to look more closely at jobs I do not get, places I cannot go, things I cannot do. For wherever barriers, detours, or disappointments exist, perhaps there is God at work, too, keeping me from falling victim to the enemy.

Therefore, Jesus said again, ... I am the gate; whoever enters through me will be saved. They will come in and go out and find pasture. The thief comes only to steal and kill and destroy; I have come that they may have life and have it to the full."
John 10:7, 9-10 (NIV)

27

CAN YOU, OR CAN'T YOU?

· · · · · · · ● ● ● ● ● ● ● ● ● · · · · · ·

Can you or can't you wear white after Labor Day? I like the crisp, clean look of white and own a number of white jackets, slacks, and tops. Yet, I hesitate to wear them after that first Monday in September.

Mom taught me that white clothing and accessories were a no-no after Labor Day, lest I be ridiculed like Fergie (Princess Sarah Ferguson of Great Britain). She made headlines in the 1990's during a trip to Texas … not because of her historic visit, but because she committed the fashion faux pas of wearing white shoes in mid-September, well after Labor Day.

So, to settle the debate, I googled Emily Post, who wrote the "bible" on fashion etiquette. And, I quote…

Then

> *Back in Emily's day – the nineteen 00s, 10s and 20s – the summer season was bracketed by Memorial Day and Labor Day. Society flocked en masse from town house to seaside "cottage" or mountain "cabin" to escape the heat. City clothes were left behind in exchange for lighter, whiter, summer outfits. Come fall and the return to the city, summer clothes were put away and more formal city clothes donned once*

more ... the signal to mark the change between summer resort clothes and clothing worn for the rest of the year was encapsulated in the dictum, "No white after Labor Day." And it stuck.

Now

Of course you can wear white after Labor Day, and it makes perfect sense to do so in climates where September's temperatures are hardly fall-like. It's more about fabric choice today than color ... The true interpretation is "wear what's appropriate – for the weather, the season, or the occasion."[3]

Further research revealed even fashion diva, Coco Chanel, wore white year-round. So, that settled the question for this Texas girl.

Hmmm, isn't it funny how we can make certain rules into hard and fast laws? Or, act on certain beliefs or traditions from habit and without question? I wonder what rules or beliefs no longer apply while I go slip into my white slacks and sandals.

CONNECTING THE DOTS

It is okay – even good sometimes – to question rules and traditions, especially those that don't make sense nor line-up with God's law of love.

God allows it. In fact, He encourages us to search His Word for what's right and what's not, rather than blindly following what someone else tells us. He set us apart from the rest of creation by giving us a mind with which to analyze and think. God intends for us to use it.

His Apostle Paul listed guidelines for how to conduct ourselves as Christians. Paul included in the list...

But examine everything carefully; hold fast to that which is good.
1 Thessalonians 5:21 (NASB)

And, the plumb line against which to determine that which is good? The Bible. We have questions. God has answers. His Word is the ultimate authority for guidance and direction. We do well to read and search it daily.

Now the Berean Jews were of more noble character than those in Thessalonica, for they received the message with great eagerness and examined the Scriptures every day to see if what Paul said was true.
Acts 17:11 (NIV)

28

THE "F" IN FAITH STANDS FOR FLEXIBILITY[4]

· · · · · · · · · ● · · · · · · · · · ·

At some point, we all experience them...one of *those* days. The ones where we want to push "Pause and Rewind" because nothing goes as planned. Where we wonder why we got out of bed in the first place. I remember one of those days...

The alarm jarred me awake. I recited my daily prayer, "Lord, this is the day You made. Let me be glad and rejoice in it." Remembering my no-time-to-breathe schedule, I added, "Lord, keep me flexible and open to Your guidance."

I should be more careful what I ask for. I thought I'd get good things and guidance. What I got was more faith and flexibility. By bedtime, I was giving thanks...

Thank You, Lord, for the garage door failing to open this morning. Rising only halfway, I couldn't back my car out and head to work. You slowed me down to take that cleansing breath of patience I needed to face an over-scheduled week. On the seventh attempt and after prayer for deliverance from the garage, You lifted the door and sent me on my way. I rejoiced and remembered...*Your power behind my persistence sees me through unexpected delays.*

And thank You, Lord, for the person who parked in my spot at work. It's like my church pew, and he — or she — trespassed in it. The unknown interloper forced me to park further away from my office entrance and extend what was already a ten-minute hike. Irritated at first, I realized by the time I opened my office door that walking the extra distance energized me with exercise I missed this morning. *Your detours have purpose.*

I appreciate the power outage that darkened and silenced everything in our office building for 20 seconds, but without customer impact. Such outages remind me how grateful I am for the convenience of electricity and generators. *Your power is sufficient.*

I'm thankful my watch battery ran out of juice mid-day. No longer able to check the time every five minutes, I quit worrying about running late. Lord, can You believe the day flowed smoothly? I handled interruptions and finished tasks at my leisure. *Your timing is perfect.*

Lastly, thank You, Lord, for slipping the magazine out of my hand when I dozed off while relaxing in the tub. Pages soaked, reading was no longer possible. I finished my bath and came to bed early. *You gave me much-needed rest.*

I closed my day with a heartfelt, "Thank You, Lord. Indeed, this was the day *You* made."

CONNECTING THE DOTS:

Plan? Yes, but then give God our agenda. Allow interruptions. They might be the Lord, ordering our tasks differently and re-constructing our schedule to ensure the right things get done according to His purpose.

Jesus reminds us that our Father is always at work (John 5:17). He is always in the midst of writing our story. Like any good story, the Author draws us in by raising the level of tension. Just when one situation resolves, another conflict comes along, and the plot takes a new twist. It keeps us turning the pages of our life, unable to put the book aside until the end.

That's why the "F" in faith stands for flexibility.

...give thanks in all circumstances; for this is
God's will for you in Christ Jesus.
1 Thessalonians 5:18 (NIV)

29

THE MESSENGER[5]

· · · · · · · ● · ● · · · · · · · ·

"Your father-in-law's condition is grave, Mrs. Johnson. Tests show more small strokes and a weakening heart. The prognosis doesn't look..." His voice trailed off. The physician glanced down to study the shine on his shoes and avoided Debbie's pleading eyes. He'd seen her look before. It searched for hope, but he had none to give.

Debbie leaned against the wall for support. She struggled for control. "There's nothing more you can do?"

"No, only keep him comfortable and pray." The doctor stared at some unseen spot on the wall behind her. "I'm so sorry." He turned and walked silently down the hallway, leaving Debbie alone to corral her thoughts.

Debbie drew a ragged breath and wondered how to tell her husband and family. *Why are Johnny and his brother out of town now? How can I tell them he's dying? God, I don't want to do this.* Debbie's thoughts raced.

She peeked through the doorway at her father-in-law, lying still beneath the white sheet. Tubes and tangled wires hooked to monitors poked out from everywhere on his body. Debbie closed her eyes, wishing she could be transported to a different place and circumstances.

She opened her eyes and sighed. Finding herself still in the hospital corridor, she turned to leave. Her shoulders slumped under the burden she carried.

The elevator door opened to the lobby. Debbie hardly remembered pushing the "down" button or stepping into the empty elevator. She moved into the hospital's main entrance and trudged toward the door.

Morning sunshine streaming through windows brightened the lobby. Three steps away from the revolving exit door, a slightly built gentleman with silver white hair stepped forward. Debbie first noticed him when he curled his fingers around her arm and pulled her to a stop.

"When you get home, read Philippians 4:13," the gentleman announced matter-of-factly.

Debbie blinked, trying to bring the stranger into focus through her moist eyes. "Excuse me?" she stammered.

"When you get home, read Philippians 4:13," he repeated, looking at her with eyes that said he saw into her soul. He smiled, dropped his hand from her arm and turned to walk away.

Whirling around after him, Debbie grabbed his arm. "Wait. Tell me what it says. I have to know *now*," she demanded, desperate for any words of hope.

The gentleman faced her and quoted the verse, "I can do all things through Him who gives me strength."

"Oh. Thank you." Debbie drew a cleansing breath and turned toward the exit again. Taking only a few steps, she turned back to thank the gentleman once more.

He wasn't there. She glanced up and down the hallway, searching for the silver-haired man who stood before her only a second ago. He'd vanished. But where?

There were no doors to duck into or corners to turn down. Only the elevator at the far end of the lobby. Its bell rang to announce its arrival. The door opened, allowing passengers to exit. No one waited to enter.

Back in her car, Debbie rested her hands on the steering wheel and pondered the silver-haired gentleman who appeared out of nowhere. His words echoed in her ears. Awareness dawned as the sun came up in the morning to push away darkness and shed light on the day. The peace that enveloped her confirmed what she now believed.

God sent Debbie a messenger, a special angel to encourage her that the Lord would provide her the power to speak the doctor's words to her father-in-law's family. God would equip her fully with *His* strength to do what she could not do alone.

And the Lord did. Just as His angel promised He would.

CONNECTING THE DOTS

Angels are real. A well-known blessing confirms that truth:

"Angels around us, angels beside us, angels within us. Angels are watching over you when times are good or stressed. Their wings wrap gently around you, whispering you are loved." ~ Angel Blessing[6]

Because they are spiritual beings, we do not always see them guiding, protecting, or delivering to us an important message from the Lord. However, they can surprise us, appearing in human form at the moment we need a word from the Lord. (See Genesis 18). Sending His angels is but one way God pours out His love and grace upon us.

Who knows whether that next stranger speaking an encouraging word to us is an angel from the Lord?

For he will command his angels concerning you to guard
you in all your ways. On their hands they will bear you up,
so that you will not dash your foot against a stone.
Psalm 91:11-12 (NRSV)

30

KEEP THE END IN MIND

· · · · · · · · · ● ● ● ● ● ● ● · · · · · ·

Try this exercise. Place two sheets of newspaper together and opened in the center. Make a long tube by rolling one corner tightly toward the opposite diagonal corner. Bend 3-4" of one end at a 90-degree angle to the rest of the tube, thus forming a small pedestal.

The test: Rest the tube's pedestal in the palm of your hand. While focusing your eyes somewhere between your palm and the middle of the tube, try to balance it upright for two minutes. What happened? My tube wobbled like Jello. My hand moved constantly, shifting six inches or more in any direction before the tube fell <30 seconds later.

Try again. Only this time, train your eyes on the top point of the tube. What happened? Was your tube steadier like mine? Did only slight hand adjustments keep it upright for two minutes or longer?

Focusing on the top end of the tube made hitting the goal easier. Why? Because we naturally sensed and made necessary adjustments to keep the whole tube upright. We focused on the end in mind.

Korah fixated on the "middle of the tube." He was a Levite and one of the chief men among Israelites exiting Egypt. But apparently not chief enough for him. Instead of concentrating on God's end in mind – getting His children to the Promised Land – Korah prioritized his desire for power and position. In the middle of the desert, he grumbled and instigated a rebellion against Moses. That self-centered, short-sighted view of circumstances cost Korah his life (Numbers 16:1-14).

I recognize Korah-moments in my past and present, too. When I feel discounted or lacking kudos, desire for reward and recognition can creep into my motivations. Buried underneath these feelings is a longing to be known. In the middle of problems or challenges, I can rush to the quickest fix to get them behind me. Hidden beneath the rushing is fear that God may not bless me for the effort. Either way, I lose sight of the long picture. Life wobbles wildly and falls prey to frustration, failure, and defeat.

CONNECTING THE DOTS

Set our hope on the long view, looking at life and circumstances with God's end in mind.

When taking this perspective, then barriers, pains, and troubles become mere steppingstones to our developing a Christ-like character and fulfilling God's eternal plan, to get every person in a right relationship with Him. As Max Lucado noted, "This is the direction in which all of history is focused. This is the moment toward which God's plot is moving. The details, characters, antagonists, heroes, and subplots all arc in this direction."[7]

Fame, personal goals, and achievements are not the end in mind. They are the "middle of the tube" compared to the true end – glorifying God in all we do. The role of our goals, works, and achievements is to build up the body of Christ (Ephesians 4:12) such that no one perishes (2 Peter 2:8-10), and all arrive at our eternal home with Christ.

Don't shuffle along, eyes to the ground, absorbed with the things right in front of you. Look up and be alert to what is going on around Christ — that's where the action is. See things from his perspective... Meanwhile, be content with obscurity, like Christ.
Colossians 3:1-2, 4 (The Message)

SECTION 4

LEARN TO LEAD LIKE JESUS

31

SMALL STEPS; BIG RESULTS

· · · · · · · ● · ● · ● · · · · · · ·

"There's got to be an easier way," I said after six phone calls and four fruitless hours hunting for resources. A typical day in the life of a hospital social worker.

I canvassed every community resource I knew to help a cancer patient pay for a piece of equipment his insurance would not cover. His family was already strapped for dollars since he missed work from the recent hospitalization.

A kernel of an idea sprang to life. *If only a fund existed for such cases.*

I pitched the suggestion to the hospital administrator who won approval to seed a small pool of dollars. We crafted a brochure – sunflower yellow with summer-grass green lettering. Marketing called it gaudy, but to me it spoke *hope, life.* The Cancer Crisis Fund was born.

With the brochure and an article in the hospital newsletter, the fund took root. Some gave ten dollars. Others, twenty-five. Occasionally a contributor sent $100.

The seed grew into a seedling. The seedling into a tree where patients and families found a moment of relief while flying into storms of chemotherapy, radiation treatments, and challenging side effects. The fund helped to buy a walker for one patient, medications for another, and next month's health care premium for a third. The Cancer Crisis Fund bridged a gap between hospitalization and discharge home where patients and families continued to wage war against disease.

When I left the hospital two years later, the fund had grown to $10,000. Three years later, contributions swelled to a California redwood-sized fund of $20,000 and served countless patients. My kernel of an idea grew into a God-sized reality.

CONNECTING THE DOTS

Never underestimate what big result God can do with small beginnings.

When nudged with an idea, however small or insignificant, only begin the work. When God is in it, we can never guess – or may never see – how small ideas prompted by His Spirit grow into trees of potential. How one word of encouragement brings a paragraph of change to one life that then overflows to many. How one simple deed compounds into a wealth of impact.

What small idea or vision has God planted in us? What holds us back from taking that first small step?

As exiled Israelites began to return home, the prophet Zechariah encouraged them, saying:

> *"Do not despise this small beginning, for the eyes*
> *of the Lord rejoice to see the work begin."*
> Zechariah 4:10 (NIV)

32
PRACTICE PENGUIN
PERSUASION

· · · · · · · · ● · ● · ● · · · · · · ·

One evening during my first year as a Director, I vented to my husband, "If my team would only do what I suggest, we wouldn't waste so much time debating the issue." Half-joking and half-serious, I admitted that I slept through the class, "How to Win Friends and Influence Others."

I regret not running across the penguin story[1] back then. It would have saved me frustrating conversations and time spent to convince someone of a better approach.

In 2003, the San Francisco Zoo housed 46 long-time resident penguins. Over the years, they grew lazy and comfortable with their daily routine... eat, rest and occasionally take a dip in their pool to cool off and keep their feathers sleek. They coasted through the day, doing only what they needed to survive.

One day, the scene changed around the penguin pool. Six new penguins moved in from Ohio, and they loved to swim. They jumped immediately into the pool and swam laps all day, rivaling the likes of Michael Phelps or Mark Spitz. They ignored and never nagged the 46 lazy penguins to join them. They just swam until evening and dragged themselves out of the pool for dinner, exhausted but content.

The original San Francisco penguins watched from the sidelines, day after day. Until one day, one of the 46 observer penguins joined the six swimmers. Then, another waddled into the water followed by three more. Before long, all 46 were in the pool with the six, flapping water on each other and lapping the pool. Without squawking a word, the six Ohio penguins persuaded the 46 land lovers to join them.

The wisdom from six persuasive penguins honed my skills of influence:

>*Lead by Example.* When challenging tradition, opposing opinions or comfortable routines, show rather than tell the new idea. Make it *my* practice first.

>*Change Team Make-up.* Introduce new members with fresh perspectives and enthusiasm or network to create partnerships outside the group. Both can shock tenured habits out of ruts and inspire new behaviors.

>*Practice Patience.* Give people the time they need — especially internal processers like myself — to consider the new approach, ask questions, and experience it for themselves. Let them modify it to make it better and make it their own.

>*And Don't Give Up.* The older the tradition or routine, the more entrenched it is. The more entrenched (and the bigger the organization), the longer it takes to influence change in behavior.

CONNECTING THE DOTS

Influence like Jesus. Pull rather than push others toward the change you want to see.

We more effectively mold culture when we lead by example, introduce fresh perspectives, practice patience, and persist. Look what one Savior and twelve ordinary men from vastly diverse backgrounds achieved using these principles. The minority can influence the majority. It just takes a little time and friendly persuasion.

Then, even if some refuse to obey the Good News, your godly lives will speak to them without any words. They will be won over by observing your pure and reverent lives.
1 Peter 3:1 (NLT)

33

A TALE OF TWO MANAGERS

A two-month stint as interim manager would help our leadership team decide who to promote to manager. Two high performing associates aspired to the one open position. Comparison found both equally matched in tenure, knowledge of the business, and achievement outcomes. The trial period would test the associates' mettle. Both would report to me.

Two weeks after the initial onboarding sessions, I sat down with the two candidates to gather their assessment of their teams and formulate development plans.

Manager wannabe #1 arrived with his pad of paper and a list of requests. His first order of business – to ask if he could order a banner with his name to display on the front of his cube. Next came requests to set up his personal phone extension and purchase business cards with his name and title, "Interim Manager." Fourth on his list of discussion topics – the assessment of his team thus far.

Two hours later, manager wannabe #2 arrived at my office. She came with a two-page document defining her goal – to help the team raise its performance. She handed me a draft approach for getting them to work together as one toward team goals and individual development plans.

Who do you think the leadership team selected for the manager job?

I appreciated wannabe #1's ambition. I, too, once set my career sights on climbing to department director, consistently achieving the highest performance ratings, and winning awards that affirmed my achievements. For more years than I care to admit, my ambition and quest for the top labored at winning personal visibility, advantage, and recognition. The ulterior motive: self-promotion that proved I was good enough and worthy.

Ambition and hard work can be a good thing. My ambition drove me to stretch my capabilities and achieve. But reaching the top did not always bring lasting satisfaction. Inevitably, the spotlight dimmed; others' expectations grew for me to produce more; and I jumped onboard to reinforce my worthiness.

That cycle looped repeatedly until I no longer enjoyed my work. Recognition and rewards were not enough to sustain the energy and passion that once drove me. Nor did they quench my thirst once and for all for a sense of personal value.

Manager wannabe #2 realized ambition's better end game ... serving others, putting their needs before ours.

CONNECTING THE DOTS

Lead like Jesus, with a servant's heart. Avoid getting caught up in the spotlight, accolades, and special privileges that may go with status.

Two ambitious brothers, James and John, once jockeyed for position, too. They petitioned Jesus outside of earshot of the other ten disciples, asking to sit at His right and left hand when He took His throne. They sought advantage, recognition, and reward for following Him those past three years.

Jesus reprimanded the two. He refocused the lens through which to view themselves and their job description as leaders, titled or not, saying:

...whoever wishes to become great among you must be your servant...
Mark 10:43 (NRSV)

Later, Paul clarified this truth when he urged the Philippians to imitate Christ's humility:

Do nothing from selfish ambition or conceit. But, in humility
regard others as better than yourselves. Let each of you look
not to your own interests but to the interests of the others.
Philippians 2:3-4 (NRSV)

34

DISCUSSION VS. DIALOGUE?

· · · · · · · · ● ● ● ● 🔘 ● ● ● ● ● · · · · · · ·

As a teenager, I discussed lots of issues with my parents. Things like chores to complete before receiving allowance, whether to date the young man I crushed on, or my readiness to strike out in driving without parental oversight. After high school graduation, discussions continued with professors and employers.

Discussion comes from the Latin word, *discussus,* meaning to dash to pieces or to scatter or shake apart. Discus, the round object hurled for distance in a track meet, originates from the same root.

That definition characterized my conversations. I hurled my discus of thoughts out there like a Greek Olympian vying for gold. To advocate my viewpoint and dash to pieces any objections or rebuttals. There was a right answer, and I had it.

Although I hurled long and hard my ideas and preferences, someone bigger and better often hurled theirs further. I lost more discussions than I won. Not so much because I held an unreasonable position, but because I failed to listen. I closed my ears to new, relevant facts or fresh perspective. Nor did I explore for common ground on which to build a better answer.

Then, I ran across an article about the art of dialogue. Coming from the Greek words, *dia* (through or across) and *logue* (discourse or talk), a dialogue is the exchange of ideas and thoughts to seek shared, mutual understanding. Quite the opposite picture of discussions. Dialogue's key differentiating element? Asking probing questions rather than hurling the discus of statements or demands.

When coaching my managers, I once challenged them only to ask open-ended, probing questions in their next one-on-one coaching session with an associate. Their goal … to guide the individual to discover the answer within themselves to grow and improve personal performance.

One tenured manager resisted, saying, "But, I know the answers and share them with my associates." He agreed to try dialogue just once only when I bargained with him. If it did not work, he could revert to his approach. But, if it did….

The manager chose his toughest associate – one he had coached on the same performance issue for the past six months. The associate would follow the manager's suggestions for about a week before slipping into old habits.

In the next 1-1, the manager replaced telling with asking a few open-ended questions instead: "*What* was the customer looking for? *How* did the customer respond when you said…? Why do you think they didn't leave the call satisfied?" And the final question: "What are three ways you could handle the situation differently to provide better service?"

After staring at each other in silence for ten minutes, the associate proffered action steps. Because they were *his* ideas and fit *his* personality, changes stuck. Two weeks evolved into two months. The associate's plan became second nature. His customer service feedback improved from average to excellent.

And the manager? He became the greatest advocate for dialogue coaching. And his team, one of the top performing.

CONNECTING THE DOTS

Engage in dialogues and avoid hurling a discus of words.

The gospels record Jesus employing dialogue with various individuals, like the woman at the well, the woman accused of adultery, or the lame man at the pool of Bethesda. With all, Jesus asked open-ended questions to find common ground through which to connect His ideas. He guided the individual to reflect upon their thoughts, feelings, and experiences with show-stopping inquiries such as:

> Who do you say I am? (Matthew 16:13-15)
> What do you want me to do for you? (Mark 10:51)
> Why are you so afraid? (Matthew 8:26)
> Why do you doubt (Matthew 15:1-2) or worry? (Matthew 6:28; Luke 12:24-36)
> Do you want to get well? (John 5:6)

And, though His message never changed, Jesus never pressed listeners for agreement or "closure." Some perceived His message at once; others needed to simmer on it before understanding. Some never got it.

That's dialogue. Interactions that seek shared connection and understanding.

Let your conversation be always full of grace, seasoned with
salt, so that you may know how to answer everyone.
Colossians 4:6 (NIV)

35

THE TIPPING POINT: GIVE UP OR GO ON?

I watched on television as four years of training and grueling practice came to an early end for medal contender Jeremy Abbott in his short program for men's figure skating. His dream to stand on the Olympic podium fell hard with him to the ice as he attempted a quadruple toe loop.

Sliding and crashing into the wall, Abbott grabbed his hip. His face contorted with pain.

Seconds passed.

Abbott winced, and then stood on his skates. Shoulders slumped in defeat as he glanced toward his coaches. They moved toward the rink's entrance door, ready to support Abbott when he hobbled off the ice, unable to finish.

A collective gasp rose from the spectators crowded into Russia's Iceberg Arena. Then applause. Vibrating, thundering applause for this young athlete's effort.

Abbott looked up and around the arena.

Then, he did the improbable. With his music still playing, Jeremy Abbott eased back into his program and completed every subsequent move and jump with Olympic precision.

The reward for his efforts? This medal contender earned 72.58 points and finished #15 in a field of 29. But, not last place. Not first, second, or third on the Olympic podium. But first in grit and perseverance after such a devastating experience.

In an interview, a reporter asked Abbott, "What happened out there?"

Abbott responded, "I heard the crowd applauding, encouraging me. I didn't want to let them down."

Did I hear that right? When tempted to give up, he heard the roars of applause and encouragement. With that wind at his back, Jeremy Abbott stared at the face of defeat and kept going.

CONNECTING THE DOTS

Who do we know at the tipping point of discouragement? Whose face is contorted in pain or shoulders slumped? Who teeters on the verge of giving up seeing no reason to continue their effort?

Encourage them. Lead like Jesus, who often encouraged others, including His confused or depressed disciples. Let others know we believe in them. Hearing our applause and encouragement may be the tipping point, the watershed moment in which they give up or go on.

So, speak encouraging words to one another. Build up hope so you'll all be together in this, no one left out, no one left behind.
1 Thessalonians 5:11 (The Message)

36

GUARD YOUR REPUTATION

· · · · · · · · ● ◉ ● · · · · · · · · ·

Jim looked forward to his annual tradition ... driving his little girl to her first day of fifth grade in a new school. Dressed in a new outfit to appease the shaky confidence that always accompanied her with change, our daughter, Jessica, climbed into Bertha.

Bertha was Jim's fifteen-year-old Dodge truck. Like Grandma, her skin was dulled with years of exposure and her upholstery worn from drivers sliding in and out under the steering wheel. Her radio mixed music with static, and her air conditioner labored to cool the cab to 72 degrees. But every morning she purred a welcome to those who relied on her for transportation.

One block from school, Jessica broke the silence within Bertha with an urgent shout, "Stop! Pull over."

Jim did and jerked toward his daughter, "What's the matter? What did you forget?"

Jessica stiff-armed Dad. Without a word, she gathered her books, opened Bertha's door, and stepped to the curb. Turning back to Dad and peering at him through her glasses, she smoothed her hair behind her ears and replied, "I'll walk from here, Daddy. I have my reputation to protect."

She slammed the door shut, turned on her heel and walked away, determined not to be seen with a parent bringing her to school, much less riding in a beat-up truck.

Jim sat stunned, mouth agape. "What reputation? You're only eleven years old."

Everyone, even an eleven-year-old, has a reputation. The business world calls it your personal brand. People draw conclusions by watching how we live out our beliefs and values in our interactions and behavior.

Reputation, or personal brand, is what people think of us because of our attitudes, actions, and words. These form their image or the feelings that swell from within when they hear our name. Ultimately, reputation is what drives others to engage with us ... or not. To choose to listen to us or not. To follow the leader in us or not.

CONNECTING THE DOTS

God made us in His image and calls us to build a reputation for holiness (Leviticus 19:2, NIV). Protect that reputation.

That's a tall order and not easy to do or sustain, as Scripture reminds us. The Israelites defiled God's image by worshipping a golden idol. Pharisees tarnished God's image with rigid laws that lost compassion in application. The New Testament church struggled to remain holy when faced with persecution for their beliefs and behaviors.

How does one build and sustain a strong reputation or brand? Not from performing holy deeds or presenting a holy demeanor alone. Outward appearances can deceive and be incongruent with what lies in truth on our hearts. Rather, our attitudes, actions, and words must flow from daily renewing of our minds to follow Christ's two greatest commandments:

> *Love the Lord your God with all your heart, all*
> *your soul and all your mind...A second is equally*
> *important: Love your neighbor as yourself."*
> Matthew 22:37 (NLT)

We have a reputation to protect as Christians, especially in leadership. We must ask often, "Do our words, deeds, and relationships remind others of Jesus? Are we fitting in with the world, or setting ourselves apart by living according to the two greatest commandments?"

> *A sterling reputation is better than striking it rich; a*
> *gracious spirit is better than money in the bank.*
> Proverbs 22:1 (The Message)

37

LOOKING FOR SHORT MEMORIES AND SECOND CHANCES

$\cdots\cdots\bullet\bullet\bullet\bullet\bullet\bullet\bullet\bullet\!\bullet\!\bullet\bullet\bullet\bullet\bullet\bullet\bullet\cdots\cdots$

For some, the topic struck a raw nerve. Questions from my presentation, "Keys to Building Personal Brand," circled a common theme...*How do I correct a mistake that left the wrong impression? How do I overcome brand-breaker moments for a brand-maker image?* Behind those questions stood individuals looking for the secret to erasing their tarnished brand; someone searching for a second chance. A do-over.

When the hour ended, eight individuals quickly queued in front of me. With downcast eyes and whispering voices, they wanted to rewrite their story in the eyes of another fixated on their brand-breaker moment or misstep. Another who was long on memory and short on forgiveness.

I pictured Jonah. Although a prophet called to carry God's message, he balked when God asked him to preach repentance to sin-city, Ninevah. Jonah's obstinacy landed him in the belly of a giant fish. There, he saw the error of his way and repented.

God gave Jonah another chance. He called Jonah a *second time* to Ninevah. This time, Jonah obeyed, Ninevah repented, and God relented, giving the city a second chance.

Happy ending, right? But, not so. Instead, Jonah was long on memory and short on forgiveness. He railed at God, "I knew it...I knew this was going to happen! That's why I ran off to Tarshish! I knew you were sheer grace and mercy, not easily angered, rich in love, and ready at the drop of a hat to turn your plans of punishment into a program of forgiveness!" (Jonah 4:1-2, The Message). Jonah wanted Ninevah destroyed for their past.

Who can blame Jonah? After all, how many times have we believed someone's promise to change only to wind up disappointed again? How many times have we seen someone drift backwards into old habits with the passage of time? Or just remain clueless or indifferent about the impact of their poor behavior?

Still, God calls us to a different answer. To grant second chances. Even to "seventy-times-seven" chances (Matthew 18:21-22).

CONNECTING THE DOTS

Forgiveness can be one of the easiest or most difficult things to do, depending on the size of the offense. Forgiving does not mean the offending person won't suffer consequences from their actions. It only means we give – or receive, if that's the case – a second chance, a do-over to do what is right.

Through the cross and blood sacrifice of Jesus, God already forgave our sins. As the offender, our required step is to sincerely repent, turn around, and live again in the model of Christ. As the offended, it is to offer grace and forgive as the Lord forgave us.

The image of those tarnished-brand seekers clung to me like sweat-soaked clothing on a humid, August day in Texas. We've all been that railing Jonah. And we've all been Ninevah, given a second chance. We must lead like Jesus and work to re-shape our approach to offenses...one *short* on memory and *long* on forgiveness.

And forgive us our debts, as we also have forgiven our debtors.
For if you forgive other people when they sin against you,
your heavenly Father will also forgive you.
But if you do not forgive others their sins,
your Father will not forgive your sins.
Matthew 6:12, 14-15 (NIV)

38

CAN THE BROKEN
BE MENDED?

· · · · · · · · · ● · ● ● · · · · · · · · ·

Have you ever tested how well frameless glasses hold up under the pressure of adults sitting on them? Let me assure you, they don't.

In an absent-minded moment I sat on those I bought only four months earlier. Earpieces once attached to the lens now dangled with exposed prongs. I wondered if they could be restored and cringed at how much repairs might cost. Adding insult to injury, it was Sunday morning. I was doomed to wear clunky, old frames until the eye-glass store opened Monday.

"How can I help you?" The technician greeted me when I walked in. I held out my mangled frames and hung my head like the child who shattered her mom's antique crystal vase while romping through the living room.

He lowered his chin and peered over his glasses. "What happened? Are you on the losing roller-derby team?"

Heat from embarrassment rushed up my neck. "I accidentally sat on them."

"Hmmm." The technician took a seat behind his worktable and pointed me toward a chair on the other side. I held my breath while he examined the broken glasses. His verdict, "This will take a while, but I think I can fix them." During the next 45 minutes, my new best friend reassembled my glasses to their original shape.

As I watched him work, I witnessed a convicting metaphor to another mangled mess I faced, but this time with an individual. Instead of butting heads with a friend over who was right or wrong, I needed to apply the technician's touch. To repair the frame through which I viewed the situation; to restore the lens through which I eyed the other person; and to mend the bridge that connected our two sides.

Completing his miracle, the technician handed me my broken glasses now made whole. Once again, I saw the world — and my next steps to heal a broken relationship — with clarity. Best of all, to my question, "How much do I owe you?" he replied, "No charge. The price has already been paid."

CONNECTING THE DOTS

Christ's sacrifice on the cross already paid the price for mending our relationship with God. We are called freely to do likewise with others. Be the one that takes that first step to build a bridge, restore a relationship.

We're bound to experience – or cause – conflict and aggravation when working with different personalities and habits. When that happens, we must consciously and intentionally take steps to mend fences, bridge gaps, and repair broken relationships. Working relationships are the groundwork to any successful effort. Leading in a way that unifies rather than divides will always yield stronger, more productive results.

Therefore, as God's chosen people, holy and dearly loved,
clothe yourselves with compassion, kindness,
humility, gentleness, and patience.
Bear with each other and forgive one another
if any of you has a grievance against someone.
Forgive as the Lord forgave you.
And over all these virtues put on love,
which binds them all together in perfect unity.
Colossians 3:12-14 (NIV)

39

THE MYTH OF
MULTI-TASKING

· · · · · · · · · · · ● · · · · · · · · · · ·

My eyes stared at the page. But my mind wandered a million miles from the couch where my daughter and I sat to read. She said something I didn't hear.

"Mmmhmmm." I mumbled.

She twisted her four-year-old body toward me. Her fingers grabbed each side of my face. She pulled me nose to nose and insisted, "Mommy, please, listen to me."

I still fight with that habit of dividing my attention. I read at the table during dinner, listen to podcasts while driving, and think of the next thing to say when others talk. I take a book to read in the tub and file my nails or glance through magazines while watching television.

I took pride in my ability to multi-task. I bought into the idea that toggling between two tasks made me more efficient and effective. I imagined that I saved time and accomplished more in the same span of minutes spent.

Quite the opposite proved true. Multi-tasking was not effective nor efficient. Really, it's a myth. An exaggerated, idealized concept that deceives us into thinking we're more productive than we are.

When I divided my attention and half-listened, the inevitable occurred. I missed something said or a facial expression that communicated the real message behind the words. I overlooked actions that revealed a clue to what was really going on. Or I failed to connect dots and see circumstances in light of a bigger picture. Worse yet, I gave another, like my child, the impression they were less important than whatever else I attended to.

Therein lies the peril, both socially and spiritually, of not staying in the moment. Of not listening with all three of my ears – the two on either side of my head and the one inside my heart. The danger of letting my mind wander rather than focus, divide rather than attend.

The solution is as simple as my four-year-old's response, "Mommy, please, listen to *me*." One thing at a time.

CONNECTING THE DOTS

What does God have to do to get our attention?

Jesus gave his full attention to each moment and each person. And, in each moment, He spoke only what the Father commanded Him to say (John 12:49).

We cannot divide our attention between the worries of this world and God. When we do, we inevitably miss those things that God reveals to us to say or do. And thus, we miss the abundant blessings and fulfilling life He has prepared for those who love Him (1 Corinthians 2:9-10).

Effective multi-tasking is a myth. To lead like Jesus, listen. Listen intentionally, singularly, and attentively. Be fully present in each moment. Then, and only then, will we hear more clearly the Holy Spirit whispering to our soul and guiding us in the way we should go.

Jesus said, *Don't worry about missing out. You'll find all your everyday human concerns will be met. Give your entire attention to what God is doing right now, and don't get worked up about what may or may not happen tomorrow. God will help you deal with whatever hard things come up when the time comes.*
Matthew 6:33-34 (The Message)

40

WHO WILL LEAD
THEM NOW?

Jason posed his dilemma as we walked across the college campus. He was President of the Finance and Business Student Societies where I headed to speak about career opportunities.

"I'm a senior business major and my officers are seniors," he explained. "We all graduate in May. We wonder, who will take the reins and lead business students after we move on?"

Jason and his officers faced one of leadership's greatest challenges ... replacing themselves when they stepped down and moved on. They looked for not just anyone but individuals who could lead the group forward. Individuals who shared the same vision and purpose of the organization, and who would expand on foundations laid by their predecessors.

Jason is not alone in his dilemma. We are all leaders of something in either our work, families, churches, or communities. The greatest test of our leadership is our *willingness* and *ability to train* another to take our position. Without a succession plan, all we accomplish can unravel. Our vision for what could be will stall or die.

In Numbers 27:22-23, Moses offers a best practice in succession planning. He knew his death approached and commissioned Joshua to lead the Israelites once he was gone. Inspired by God, Moses chose Joshua based on three critical "P's" -- potential, passion, and preparation.

> *Potential:* Early in the exodus, Moses observed Joshua's leadership potential when he led the Israelite army to fight and defeat the Amalekites. Joshua excelled in his role. Several times he led the nation to victories over its enemies (Exodus 17:9).

> *Passion:* Moses also knew Joshua trusted God with a passion. He listened as Joshua and Caleb returned from a spy mission to the promised land and encouraged Israelites to enter it as God directed. When the ten other spies grumbled that its inhabitants were too powerful to fight, Joshua and Caleb tore their clothes and pleaded with the Israelites to reconsider and not rebel against God's plan (Numbers 14:1-9).

> *Preparation:* Moses selected Joshua as his assistant, giving Joshua firsthand experience to understand what it meant to lead God's people. Only Joshua accompanied Moses part way up the mountain when Moses received the ten commandments. Other references show him often at Moses' side.

Like Moses, Jesus chose his disciples by who could carry forward the vision to "... go and make disciples of all nations" (Matthew 28:19, NIV). He chose them not for their status and skills, but for their potential and passion. And then He spent three years preparing them for the day He knew would come...the day they would lead, spreading the message of the Kingdom into the world. Granted, one disciple opted out by choice. But the remaining eleven (and one recruit) ignited a movement that still grows today around the world.

CONNECTING THE DOTS

Whether leading at work, in a community, our families, or churches, we must reflect and plan intentionally to pass our values, beliefs, and wisdom to the next generation of leaders. That's one responsibility in advancing God's kingdom here on earth.

When choosing who can succeed us, look beyond outer appearances, status, and current skills. With the Holy Spirit as guide, choose like Moses and Jesus. Consider our successor's potential, passion, and response to preparation.

Each of us is only one dot in the bigger picture God is painting. So, who is our Joshua? Who will carry the banner forward after we graduate to the next season of a job or life? Who should we help mentor and prepare now as the next dot in God's march to the end of history? His-story.

Then Moses summoned Joshua and said to him in the presence of all Israel, "Be strong and courageous, for you must go with this people into the land that the Lord swore to their forefathers to give them ... The Lord himself goes before you and will be with you.
Deuteronomy 31:7-8 (NIV)

SECTION 5

FAITH WORDS
TO GROW BY

41

STAND ON THE PROMISES[1]

· · · · · · · · ● · ● · · · · · · · · ·

Definition: to have a certain position or location; to maintain one's position, as an army stands its ground rather than retreat.

synonyms: abide · fix in place · adhere to · hold on.[2]

We all experience them at one time or another ... broken promises. Some unfulfilled on purpose. Others, unintentionally. A few, we may still hold out hope to be kept.

I remember times of grief and loneliness from broken promises in relationships. But I also remember later, standing at God's altar with the man who promised to have me, hold me, and love me. And he has, even when I fall short.

After worrying about remaining childless, I remember standing by a baby crib, amazed the tiny bundle sleeping there was my newborn daughter. Then sixteen years later I prayed for her safety as she backed out of the garage and onto the streets solo for the first time. I remember thanking God every night she opened the back door to let me know, "I'm home!"

I remember the car accident when I found myself on the pavement in the middle of five o'clock traffic wondering where my car went. And I remember the emergency room where the doctor pronounced that I escaped injury with nothing more than torn pantyhose and a ripped dress.

> If one of His promises does not work out one way, we can trust God will work it some other way we cannot yet see.

I remember standing in disbelief when I didn't get the promotion, I was certain was rightfully mine. Then, I remember later standing in my new employer's office, stunned yet thrilled with the "better-than-I-could-ever-imagine" opportunity that opened to me.

I remember standing at the foot of my father's bed when the doctor said he had a disabling heart condition but could live four to five years if he took care of himself. Then, I remember standing at the foot of his grave *seventeen* years later, flooded by the precious time and memories God gifted me since his diagnosis.

CONNECTING THE DOTS

We can stand on God's promises.

Through every twist and turn in life, in each joy and sorrow, mountain or valley, I realized I stood on promises. I still stand on them today.

Not promises that everything will always turn out the way *I* want, but on the promise of God's love and faithfulness. His promise to always be with me and for me, to guide and deliver me through it all. His promise to weave all things to good.

God's will and the outcomes He promises are fixed. Yet, His ways are fluid.[3] Because of free will, people and circumstances can thwart God's plan, but not His promises. If one of His promises does not work out one way, we can trust God will work it another way we cannot yet see. We can find many scriptural examples, from Abraham finding a wife for Isaac (Genesis 24:1-9) to Christ's crucifixion and resurrection.

God keeps His promises. In the words of R. Kelso Carter's beloved hymn, I am...

Standing on the promises that cannot fail,
when the howling storms of doubt and fear assail,
by the living Word of God, I shall prevail,
standing on the promises of God.[4]

I am with you, and I will protect you wherever
you go...I will not leave you until I have finished
giving you everything I have promised you.
Genesis 28:15 (NLT)

42

SOMEWHERE OVER THE RAINBOW: HOPE

· · · · · · · ● ● ● ⬤ ● ● ● · · · · · · ·

Definition: the expectation for a certain thing to happen

synonyms: expectation · confidence · faith ·
trust · belief · conviction · assurance[5]

My husband slammed the pot onto the stove as I walked through the back door. From the hallway I spotted the telltale red blotches on his face and neck — the ones that signaled either a major event or crisis.

"What's going on, Jim?" I strained to keep my voice even against a foreboding that hung in the air.

"Carol's doctor called today." Jim's sister suffered chronic health problems since she was a teenager. For the last six months, those problems landed her more in than out of hospitals. Five days ago, she was in.

"She can't care for herself alone anymore. He suggested a nursing home, and ..." Jim's voice took a sarcastic tone, "he's ready to discharge her this coming Monday." Four days away.

The next morning my husband and I fell silent over breakfast. We were exhausted over questions we had debated late hours into the night.

How would we find a suitable place over a weekend? With Carol's complicated medical history, who would admit her? What if she refused to go? And how would her meager savings stretch to cover costs?

No answers popped to mind. Not last night. Not this morning.

I retreated to the bedroom to dress for work. While staring into the mirror, wishing it were a crystal ball with magical solutions floating to the surface, another problem pressed its way into my thoughts. Uneasiness about a downward spiraling economy raised concerns about layoffs. A recent announcement at the office confirmed the inevitable.

Queasiness rippled through my stomach. I shook my head, trying to throw away that worry. Another one took its place.

"Jim, I almost forgot. Did I get a letter from my sister yesterday? She sent me her check to register for the ladies retreat we plan to attend."

"I put it in your spot on the breakfast table. Didn't I?" Jim rummaged through stacks of paperwork he sorted at the table the previous day. No letter. No check.

He retraced his steps. "It arrived. I put it at your spot on the breakfast table. But that's the last I remember it. Worrying about Carol, who knows where I put it."

Carol, work, a lost check. My frustrations gave way to hopelessness around problems without ready answers. I left my spouse rummaging through the trash in search of the elusive check while I gathered my tote and headed for work.

The early morning darkness matched my gloomy mood. My stomach was in knots from twisting troubles back and forth in my mind. My shoulders sagged under burdens piling up. And it wasn't even 8 a.m. yet.

Needing to refocus on something less stressful, I shifted my thoughts to my upcoming Sunday school lesson. My topic was the fourth fruit of the Spirit — patience. *How timely is that?* I wondered. *I could use some about now.*

I lingered on an idea in the study...*hope inspires patience in circumstances.* "So, that's why I'm short on patience — loss of hope," I mused out loud.

The Greek word for *hope, elpis,* translated as the expectation of something good — not the "trying to think positively so something good might happen" type of hope, but the "expectation it actually will occur."

The nuance caught my imagination. An email last night referenced Psalm 30. "Funny," I chuckled, "a psalm with a theme of hope." My shoulders straightened slightly.

Just as promised — my growing hope inspired my heart to swell with accompanying patience. My mood lightened. I sensed the increasing volume of an inner voice saying, "Hold on. Something better *is* around the corner."

With my drive ending, I made the final turn toward the parking garage. I prayed for more patience inspired by *elpis* hope — hope that would guide the firm safely through troubled economic times, hope that my sister-in-law's impossible situation resolved favorably, and hope my husband found that lost check.

As I approached the parking garage entrance, God's answer caught the corner of my eye. In the dusky light of dawn, it rose boldly into the sky and arched sharply over the building's upper deck — a rainbow. Thick ribbons of color illuminated through the darkness. Vibrant braids of red, yellow and green shimmered against the velvet blue sky as a reminder of God's covenant with all of life upon earth. The rainbow, the symbol of hope and expectation that God *always* delivered His people (see Genesis 9:12-16).

I laughed out loud. Only God could put a rainbow in the sky on a perfectly dry day.

God validated that hope the rest of the day. The first hints of success in meeting targets at work eased performance pressures. My hubby greeted me at home with more good news. The doctor decided to keep his sister longer to stabilize her condition. The reprieve bought us time to find the right place.

Then, as if to punctuate, circle, and underscore the message of His morning rainbow, God reinforced it one last time that evening. While cleaning out a magazine holder, I came across a bookmark buried beneath a stack of books. One word lay inscribed on an ivory background in a rainbow of color.

The word? *HOPE!*

God ended my day as He began it — with hope. The *elpis* kind of hope that inspired patience. Patience that allowed me to wait, trusting in the Lord's faithfulness with my circumstances.

Oh, and that pesky lost check? I patiently waited with certain hope it would appear. As expected, it surfaced three months later. Attached to a discount coupon my husband had tucked away in the pantry for future use. I hoped the check was somewhere, only momentarily hidden from view, like so many answers to life's dilemmas.

CONNECTING THE DOTS

Expect the Lord to deliver hope to the hopeless. Remember, He is faithful. He's delivered us before. He will do it again and again. Lean into life's struggles expecting His promised hope. Hope that inspires patience to wait for Him.

> *Yet I still dare to hope when I remember this:*
> *The faithful love of the Lord never ends!*
> *His mercies never cease.*
> *Great is his faithfulness;*
> *his mercies begin afresh each morning.*
> Lamentations 3:21-23 (NLT)

43

THE LOOK OF FORGIVENESS

· · · · · · · · ● ● ◉ ● ● · · · · · · · · ·

Definition: process of canceling a debt; act of letting go of feeling angry or resentful toward someone for an offense, flaw, or mistake.

synonyms: absolution · exoneration · mercy · reprieve · pardoning[6]

I was a straight-A student and not-so-humble fifteen-year-old when an Italian couple hired me to help in their bakery. My first customer of the day pointed to a display case stocked with chocolate glazed donuts. "I'll take a dozen."

I stooped, pulled the tray toward me, and rested it on my knee. The first and second donuts made it into the white paper bag. On the third, I lost my balance. Grabbing the counter to steady myself, the tray slid off my knee and flipped upside down, clanging louder on the tile floor than a fire station's alarm bell. Twenty donuts lay smashed beneath the pan. I chased the last one as it rolled across the floor to rest on top of the Italian wife's foot.

Pushing back the hairnet that slid over my eyes during the chase, I swiped at the chocolate smeared across my white apron. "Let me see if there's more in the back," I said.

Anxious to escape, I turned and shoved through the kitchen's swinging doors, without looking through their small round window to the other side.

Thumpf. The baker's pan of strawberry bear claws sailed across the room.

"Ohmygosh. I'm so sorry," I said, grabbing rolls off the floor.

"Don't worry," the baker reassured me. "I'm baking more." Then, he pointed to two decorated cakes sitting near the industrial-sized ovens. "Here, carry these out front and box them."

With one cake poised on each palm, I opened the left swinging door with my hip and shoved the right side with my foot. The chocolate birthday cake made it through unscathed. The triple-tiered, wedding one did not. The swinging door snapped backwards like a sling shot, crushing butter cream roses, and slicing a one-inch wedge out of the bottom tier. I stared at the cake with eyes widened to the size of donuts. I had cost the baker a chunk of his livelihood, and the morning was still young.

The baker reached for the damaged cake. In a voice warmer than the oven-heated air that smelled of fresh-baked bread, he said, "Here. Give it to me. I can fix it like new. Go help customers." With the wave of his hand, the baker forgave me. He sent me back to work, free to do what he hired me to do.

CONNECTING THE DOTS

Forgiveness frees us to start anew; allows us to move forward. Forgiving others frees them to do likewise.

Try as we may to be perfect, we make mistakes and messes. That's human nature. The Apostle Paul understood this all too well. He said, "I want to do what is right, but I can't. I want to do what is good, but I don't. I don't want to do what is wrong, but I do it anyway" (Romans 7:18-19, NLT). Sound familiar?

Jesus' sacrifice changed everything. God, in His mercy and through the cross, pardoned our sin-debts. Those big and small; past, present, and future. He restored our relationship with Him. He freed us to start anew.

Pharisees brought to Jesus a woman caught in adultery. They wanted to stone her to death in accordance with the Law. Jesus responded, "Okay, let the one who never sinned cast the first stone." Slowly, the crowd dropped their stones and slipped away. Finding no one remained to condemn her, Jesus turned and said, "Neither do I condemn you; go and sin no more" (John 8:11, NKJV). Jesus forgave and freed the woman to start anew.

That's what God's forgiveness of us looks like. That's what our forgiveness of others looks like.

Be kind and compassionate to one another, forgiving
each other, just as in Christ God forgave you.
Ephesians 4:32 (NIV)

44

GIVE

· · · · · · · · · · ● · · · · · · · · · ·

Definition: freely transfer the possession of
(something) to (someone); hand over to

synonyms: provide · furnish with · offer ·
bestow upon · contribute to [7]

Nothing special happened the day my husband announced, "We need to start tithing." He was reading his Bible that morning, a habit he developed when attending a Disciple 1 Bible study series.

"Okay," I said, "but what made you come to that conclusion?"

"God said so," he replied simply. "Like right here in Deuteronomy: 'You shall go there, bringing there your burnt offerings and your sacrifices, your tithes, and your donations'" (Deuteronomy 12:6, NRSV).

We believed *every good thing given and every perfect gift is from above* (James 1:17, NASB). We knew it intellectually, but never committed to giving back a certain part of our gifts on a consistent basis. We regularly put a random amount of dollars in the Sunday offering plate, but we never committed to nor pledged anything specific.

Jim and I had reached a crossroads in our discipleship. That day, tithing became a deliberate line item in the family budget. We adjusted our spending to make available a small tithe.

After a year, we discovered we never missed the tithed money nor felt deprived. And, God always provided. Sometimes, in the form of unanticipated checks to cover an unforeseen expense. Other times, His provision was not obvious but just as real. Such as when our eight-year old car with 90,000 miles lasted another four years and 60,000 miles before it died. Or our home's air conditioner whose life span stretched from the norm of 10-15 years to 27 years.

After that first year, as possible, Jim and I adjusted our spending to allow for additional increases in our tithe and giving to charitable causes. We intentionally set aside a percentage of income for our budget's charitable giving bucket. As our giving increased, so did our joy.

Our growth in giving is not yet finished. R. G. LeTourneau (1888-1969) a Christian and wealthy industrialist, reached the point in his life of giving 90 percent of his income to the Lord. As he put it, "It's never a question of how much I will give, but a question of how much I will keep."

CONNECTING THE DOTS

To give generously means to steward all our God-given time, talent, gifts, and resources such that our life reflects that we "Seek first the kingdom of God and His righteousness."

Practicing Biblical generosity calls us to take steps to adjust spending and to draw closer to God, such as...

...explore what the Bible says about giving and why. Start by reading what Jesus says in Matthew 25:14-30; Matthew 13:44-47; and Luke 12:32-34.

...attend a course in financial stewardship.

...determine to fast from one item of spending during Lent and contribute that money to church or a community ministry.

...work with our allowance or budget to decide how to move towards giving a tithe (10% of income) by increasing current giving.

In everything I did, I showed you that by this kind of hard work we must help the weak, remembering the words the Lord Jesus himself said: "It is more blessed to give than to receive."
Acts 20:35 (NIV)

45

GO (IN RADICAL HOSPITALITY)

· · · · · · · · · ● ● ● ● ● ● ● ● ● ● · · · · · · ·

Definition: move from one place or point to another; leave; depart

synonyms: move · proceed · make one's way
· advance · progress · become[8]

After my husband and I missed five straight weeks of attending church, three members of our Sunday school class each sent an email or card on three consecutive days. All contained the same sentiment, "We miss you. Are you okay?"

My tears came unexpectedly. A painful memory pushed its way to the surface.

I was eleven years old and walking to class with my best friend. Suddenly, she turned to me and said matter-of-factly, "I can't be your friend anymore. I'm going to be friends with Mary." She whirled around and weaved her way through the crowded hallway, hailing Mary to wait up.

I don't know how long I stood there in silence. Other fifth and sixth graders jostled past me while I strained to grasp what just happened. I only knew my best friend severed the moorings that anchored my fragile sense of belonging and left me adrift and alone.

I no longer belonged. Until a few months later…

In that same hallway, Sherrie reached out to me. I don't know why Sherrie moved away from her usual circle of friends that day to walk with me. I was a shy, geeky eleven-year-old who wore glasses compared to her socially outgoing, attractive, and confident personality. Yet, her act of kindness drew me from a lonely, self-conscious existence into a blossoming friendship that spanned seven years.

Sherrie sat by me at lunch where we laughed at each other's jokes. We bemoaned gym class together. We plotted how to get our moms to let us shop the mall alone. She admired my new clothes and invited me to her birthday party.

When my family moved three states away, Sherrie threw me a surprise going-away party. We kept up correspondence through high school, but eventually lost contact during college, as life took us down different roads.

Three notes from our Sunday school class reminded me of Sherrie and the importance of hospitality. Stepping outside of one's circle can extend a needed welcome to a stranger or someone different. One act of such kindness can encourage another to "mount up with wings like eagles" with strength to carry on. The hospitality from the class reminded me, I belong.

CONNECTING THE DOTS

Go – that's how our faith is lived out. The world needs Jesus and Jesus needs us to invite someone to belong. Go out into the world with radical hospitality to all who cross our paths. Consider committing to…

>…call someone we haven't seen in a while and let them know we miss them. Ask if there is anything they need.

>…pray about who we could invite to church or an activity they might enjoy. Then, invite whoever comes to mind.

>…reach out to the one who sits alone or apart on the playground, at work, or on a bench while others select sides and join in the game.

>…invite someone to lunch just to get to know them better. Ask questions about background and interests, and then connect them with opportunities to engage in related groups or activities.

>…find someone at school, work, or our community who is unlike ourselves and reach out to them in a way that reflects God's love. Accept them as they are.

Lord, when was it that we saw you a stranger and welcomed you?
… and when was it that we saw you in prison and visited you?
Matthew 25:38 (NRSV)

46

DIVINE PROVIDENCE: MORE THAN COINCIDENCE

· · · · · · · · · · ● · · · · · · · · · · · ·

Definition: God providing protective or spiritual care.

synonyms: fate · destiny · God's will · divine
intervention · serendipity[9]

My eyes settled on his easy grin. He threw his head back with a bellowing laugh that resonated across the room, holding onto the joke his friend told. He towered above his circle of friends but hunched his shoulders slightly forward as if trying to mask the full height of his 6'3" frame.

I shuddered wanting to shake my attraction to those warm green eyes and spirited laugh. I was not ready for another trampled heart. One still rested in my chest, mangled from a breakup four months earlier.

Fresh out of graduate school and in a new city, I needed a few friends to bridge my loneliness. Nightclubbing was not my scene, so I joined a church singles class the size of Texas. I preferred a root canal to walking into the room of four hundred strangers every week, but how else would I meet new acquaintances?

Pushing past my shyness, I meandered over to the class's regular Wednesday night gathering where they flocked to dance and get to know one another. Within an hour I depleted my conversation starters. My desire to fit in took a backseat to my fear of awkward beginnings with new people. I pushed off the wall, ready to bolt for the solitude of my apartment.

His easy grin drew me back. With unusual boldness, I approached the young man and his friend, and introduced myself.

"Hi, I'm Gloria."

"I'm Jim." His voice could melt icicles on a wintry day.

Jim's friend caught the eye of another group and drifted away to join them. Jim remained, and I lost track of time as we eased into teasing banter. But, thirty minutes later my ballooning confidence burst. Our interaction ended abruptly when a young woman interrupted and asked Jim, "Wanna dance?"

"Sure," he agreed. With a nod in my direction, Jim strolled to the dance floor.

Well, so much for that. Nausea crept into my gut along with anger born out of what I considered his rude exit. I squared my shoulders, wove my way through laughing couples, and left for home.

Sunday rolled around. I braced for another "worse-than-a-root-canal" hour with the singles class. Putting on a smile, I ventured into the feeding frenzy of networking with several hundred potential friends.

Still smarting from Wednesday's rejection, the last person I wanted to see was Jim. The first person to catch my eye and take a seat behind me as class began was...Jim.

As the lesson ended, groups formed caravans to lunch. An icicle-melting voice called out to me, "Hey, what happened to you Wednesday night?"

"Nothing. I was tired and left." I bit off each word.

"Going to lunch with everyone now?"

"No. Plans."

"Then how about a movie later?"

"Can't today. Plans."

"Okay. If you change your mind, I live at the Trails. Across the street from your place, I think. Several of us are getting together at the pool."

With a cursory nod, I turned on my heels and left for my other pressing plans — a solo lunch at the apartment, grocery shopping, dusting furniture.

The afternoon lumbered forward. In a fit of restlessness, I grabbed my bike and told myself I wanted to get exercise. Part truth. Full truth, that icicle-melting voice beckoned me. I pushed out the door before I could change my mind. Without thinking, I steered toward the Trails Apartments across the street.

I'm not sure what I distinguished first – his distinctive laugh or his tanned, broad shoulders lounging by the pool. Swallowing anxiety, I rode over to him.

"Hi, Gloria," his baritone voice melted my icicled resistance. Conversation came easy for hours before I accepted his final invitation to the movies.

"Great show," Jim declared, taking hold of my elbow and guiding me through the exiting crowd. "How about a bite to eat before I take you home? Denny's should still be open."

Within minutes, we slid into the booth, gave the waitress our orders, and began the mating dance.

"Where are you from?" Jim led with a typical "getting-to-know-you" question. "You don't talk with that Texas drawl to be from here."

"I was born in Dallas, but my family moved around the Midwest while I was growing up. When I was fourteen years old, we moved to Kansas City."

"Hey, I lived in Kansas City, too. Moved there in '67. Went to Shawnee Mission East High School."

"Really? Me, too." Surprised by the fluke in our histories, I calculated the math in my head. "We just missed each other. We moved to Omaha in '66."

"Where did you live in Kansas City?" Jim probed further.

"On Cambridge Street in Prairie Village. And you?"

"Now that's a coincidence. My family bought a home about two miles from there. How'd you get back to Dallas?"

"A lot of family still lives here. After finishing graduate school in May of '73, I moved back for my first job. At St. Paul Hospital...where I was born, of all things. Moved into an apartment around Forest Lane and Josey."

Jim relaxed back in the booth, cocked his head slightly and stared at me for about ten seconds. "Really? My parents moved to Dallas in '73. Bought a home hardly a mile from your apartment. I moved home in May of '73, after I graduated from college. I'm surprised we never ran into each other at the grocery store or something."

Silence followed as we mulled over the links in our stories.

Jim interrupted my thoughts, "So, how did you get from North Dallas to your current apartment?"

"I needed more space but affordable. This place fits the bill. Moved there May, '74. And you?"

"Yes, moved to the Trails Apartments in May of '74. It was time to get my own place."

"Ohmygosh," I whispered. Then, regaining composure, "I guess you chased me all over the Midwest until you caught up with me, huh?"

That afternoon, Jim and I journeyed the last serendipitous mile of moves that brought us geographically closer over thirteen years. Thus, began a relationship that culminated in marriage eighteen months later.

CONNECTING THE DOTS

God works for the long-term good of our welfare. He often does so in and through events that may seem unrelated at the time and through people He places in our paths. What we call coincidence is often God's Providence. Jim and I coming together is one glimpse of His divine intervention. We find two other biblical examples in the stories of Ruth and Esther.

Reasons for such happenings and chance meetings may not be realized for months or years, if ever. Our role is to flow with Him, to trust that each step of the journey intersects us with the life to which God calls us for His eternal purpose - to reconcile all things to Himself (Colossians 1:20).

For I know the plans I have for you, declares the Lord, plans
for welfare and not for evil, to give you a future and a hope.
Jeremiah 29:11 (NIV)

47

HAVE WORD, WILL TRAVEL

· · · · · · · · · · ● ● ● ● ● ● ● ● ● ● · · · ·

Definition: The Bible or a part of it

synonyms: Bible · Scripture · Holy Word
· Holy Book · Word of God[10]

One of television's Westerns told of a hired gun named Paladin. His calling card read, *Have Gun, Will Travel.* The show's theme song described him as a "knight without armor in a savage land, who travels wherever he must." We, too, are called to be knights, but with spiritual armor, in a savage land; called to travel where we must, not with a gun, but with the Word.

Jim's sister never used the devotional Bible she bought from Christian Book Distributors. I found it while helping Jim close out her apartment after deteriorating health forced her to move into a nursing facility. Still wrapped in cellophane, the Bible rested on the bottom of a box beneath two other unopened books. Since it couldn't squeeze into my sister-in-law's new living arrangements, the Word traveled to our home where I placed it on my office bookshelf. There, it rested, unopened and gathering thin sheets of dust.

Two years later, after hearing about the practice of trying different Bible translations each year, I remembered the devotional Bible. The cellophane came off, and I went for a fresh look at God's Word. Its simple language and *Life Lessons* in the margins stirred new insights. Articles about *Christ Through the Bible* pointed to His presence in the Old Testament as well as the New. I was hooked and profited spiritually.

During lunch with my sister one day, the conversation turned to the new Bible. My contagious excitement traveled straight to her heart. She went home and ordered a copy for herself.

Two weeks later my sister found a like-new copy of the same Bible for $2 while shopping in an outlet store. She texted, asking if I knew anyone who might enjoy it. I did, so she purchased it for me to pass along.

That copy traveled to a young woman in our Bible study. New to studying the Word, she found Scripture confusing and hard to read. "I think you'll find this one easier to understand," I reassured her.

Almost two years later, the young woman commented to a mutual friend, "Did you know Gloria gave me a Bible? I love, love, love it. I read it every day now." The young woman's excitement roused the interest of another friend. That person traveled to the store and purchased a copy for herself.

Six months later, I shared in another group how this one Bible[11], ordered but never used by my sister-in-law, traveled and bore good fruit, nevertheless. After class, a friend texted me, "Which Bible was that? I want to get a copy."

Have Word, Will Travel, traveled on.

CONNECTING THE DOTS

Be a messenger of the Word. Pass it along whenever, wherever, and in whatever form best fits the moment.

The Apostle Paul proclaimed, "Therefore, we are ambassadors for Christ, God making his appeal through us" (2 Corinthians 5:20, ESV). Being an ambassador for Christ can take many forms. Sometimes our Christ-imitated behavior tells the story. Other times we share meaningful Scripture that fits the moment or need. Or we can just pass along a translation of the Bible that engaged us in a fresh way.

Whichever the case, let our calling card say, *Have Word, Will Travel*. Be a messenger of the Word. God will take care of the rest.

Just as rain and snow descend from the skies and don't go back until they've watered the earth, Doing their work of making things grow and blossom, producing seed for farmers and food for the hungry, So will the words that come out of my mouth not come back empty-handed. They'll do the work I sent them to do, they'll complete the assignment I gave them.
Isaiah 55:10-11 (The Message)

48

CHURCH

· · · · · · · · ● ● ● ◉ ● ● ● ● · · · · · ·

Definition: whole body of Christian believers, professing
the same creed and acknowledging the same ecclesiastical
authority; a building for public worship of God

synonyms: faith community · the Lord's
house · movement · communion[12]

In one of my favorite Charlie Brown cartoons, Snoopy is lying on
his back staring at the clouds, asking, "I wonder – is life a multiple-
choice test or a true/false?" In the next frame, a voice comes out of the
clouds and replies, "I hate to tell you this, but it's a 1,000-word essay!"

For years I viewed "church" as a true/false question: Do you
attend? True or false? Until we joined a small community church
where the 1,000-word essay unfolded.

My first Sundays there reminded me of my teen years. Dad
received promotions that moved us away from our hometown in
Texas to the Midwest. Anyone who's lived in or around Kansas City,
Omaha, or Des Moines knows their wintry mornings. As you rush
to your car, your breath catches from the cold and biting winds only
to find windshields frozen over.

If you're a Texas, thin-blooded gal like me and in a hurry, first instinct is to throw a pan of boiling water on the windshield. But Dad warned me against such impatience. So, I sat, teeth chattering, and turned on the defroster.

Periodically, I gunned the motor, certain the faster the engine went, the faster it heated. Eventually the engine warmed, and the defroster threw out toasty air. And a pinpoint of cleared glass appeared on the bottom of the windshield.

Those first Sunday mornings at our new church carried me back to that car, trembling from the cold of not knowing anyone, having left friends in the last neighborhood. My motor raced with spiritual impatience to melt the frost so I could get to wherever God wanted me to go. "Wait on the Lord" was not in my DNA. Neither could I see clearly what lay ahead.

It began at the bottom of my heart's window with tiny beginnings of a peephole that slowly enlarged as we experienced the warm welcome of a Sunday school class. People opened to support us and share the difficulties of parenting an only child. Somewhere along the line, a nine-month Disciple Bible study melted me to the realization God was actively working in my life, equipping me for days ahead.

I idled that first year, letting the church body's love melt the spiritual chill that had settled within me. However, one can't idle forever. The car either stalls, or we die from exhaust fumes.

At some point, the windshield clears enough to shift gears and back out of the driveway. With the encouragement our new church provided, the time came for me to "back out of the driveway" and steer forward in faith that I, too, had a contribution to make.

Someone asked me to join the children's council, lead the adult ministry council, and teach a Sunday school class. I gave out handfuls of candy at the children's Halloween party and went to administrative board meetings to debate the need for building a new sanctuary. I was in the road, merging into the life of the church.

Since then, we moved and changed church families several times. While the building and faces changed, the experience of church did not. I went, feeling chilled by the unfamiliar. But I anticipated the tiny opening on the windshield of my heart would grow in time. Sure enough, it expanded. Not in church as a true/false question, but in the warmth of church as a 1,000-word essay in the body of Christ.

CONNECTING THE DOTS

From the beginning, *The Lord God said, "It is not good for the man to be alone"* (Genesis 2:18, NIV). God created us to live in relationship with one another. He intends for us to work and grow as a church. A body of Christian believers – diverse members but unified under the power and authority of one Spirit (Ephesians 4:4).

Seeing our way forward is difficult alone. God meant for us to find and join a body of believers with and through whom we can spur one another into a deeper relationship with Him, bundled in the warmth of church fellowship.

And let us consider how we may spur one another on toward love and good deeds, not giving up meeting together, has some are in the habit of doing, but encouraging one another – and all the more as you see the day approaching.
Hebrews 10:24-25 (NIV)

49

WHEN LIFE WEARS YOU DOWN, REST

· · · · · · · · · ● · ● · ● · ● · · · · · · ·

Definition: cease work in order to relax, refresh oneself,
or recover strength; *(music)* an interval of silence

synonyms: relax · ease up/off · let up · slow
down · pause · be propped up by[13]

When I traveled to Tucson for a meeting, I joined six other
individuals for an excursion through the desert in an open-aired jeep.
Decked in a stark white tank top, navy blue shorts, and jean-colored
tennies, I slathered my pale legs with #30 sunscreen, donned my visor,
and grabbed two bottles of water before climbing into the back seat.

Four hours later, I returned with pink cheeks, red kneecaps, and
coated with enough sand to fill a sandbox for the neighbor's child.
My white top was brown and my navy shorts ivory.

With those two bottles of water long since consumed and sweated
out in the 112-degree heat, I staggered into the resort lobby, filthy and
desperately thirsty. Someone saved me with an ice-cold glass of water.
Refreshed, I headed to my room in search of a nap and to wash the
desert's grit down the drain.

Life sometimes wears me down as surely as the desert sun depleted my energy. The heat of battling opposition and unexpected circumstances can tire me out. That's why one Sunday, after a particularly pressure-filled week of work and family crises, I shut off my alarm and pulled the pillow over my head to block sunlight streaming through our window. Physically and mentally drained, I hollered to my husband, "I'm attending 'church of the covers' this morning."

"You can't," Jim reminded me. "Don't you have a meeting after church?" Oh, yeah. I shook cobwebs from my brain, washed sleep from my eyes, and hurriedly dressed.

Feeling dusty, thirsty, and frazzled from the week's demands, I melted into the pew. My soul thirsted for the cool water of God's renewing Spirit.

> Retreat and restoration are not an indulgence nor are they optional, especially when traveling through the deserts of life.

The time connecting with others and God, both handed me the equivalent of that ice-cold glass of refreshing water. His Words from the pulpit ceased my worries and propped me up with renewed strength. Worship songs washed the grit of the week's difficulties down the drain. Smiles and hugs from fellow worshippers shored up my sagging spirit. Two hours later, I walked back into the world rested and refreshed.

CONNECTING THE DOTS

When life wears us down – or to avoid it wearing us down – we must pause and rest. Retreat and time for restoration are not an indulgence nor optional, especially when traveling through the deserts of life.

God calls us to rest. His Word is filled with promises to provide rest, just as "He rested from all the work of creating that he had done" (Genesis 2:3, NIV). Even Jesus called to His followers, "Come to me, all you who are weary and burdened, and I will give you rest" (Matthew 11:28, NIV).

The Hebrew word for Sabbath means to cease, stop, or rest. Long stretches of work without breaks only stress and exhaust us. Periodic pauses refresh the mind, body, and soul. Rest replenishes mental resources and helps us become more productive and creative.

Bottom line: Take regular rest stops during the day, week, or desert seasons of life. Purposefully build in an interval of silence or a change of pace or activity. And the best place to rest? With and in the Lord.

> *The Lord replied, "My Presence will go with*
> *you, and I will give you rest."*
> Exodus 33:14 (NIV)

50

REVELATION: DID I MISS HER?

Definition: making known something previously unknown; divine or supernatural disclosure of something relating to human existence or the world.

synonyms: disclosure · declaration · utterance · announcement · divulgence[14]

I arrived at our get-together fifteen minutes early. Not seeing my friend at the restaurant's outside patio tables, I walked inside to scan the lunch crowd already gathering. Still no friend. So, I requested a window table for two, grabbed a seat and waited...and waited...and waited.

After previewing the menu and making a mental note of my selection, I checked my calendar. *Yep, right day, time, and place. I'll call her.* That's when the image flashed — of my cell phone sitting on the dining table, recharging. So, I waited some more and passed time making a "To Do" list and eavesdropping on animated conversations at the next table.

It wasn't like her to not show up without calling. But, after waiting an hour, I gave up, paid for my iced tea, and exited the restaurant.

As I snaked my way through the now-crowded outside patio, I spotted my friend. Sitting behind a large round concrete pole. Sipping a tea, reading a paperback, waiting for me. She was there all along. I had missed her arrival while waiting inside the restaurant, distracted and head down in the corner.

Now, when I meet my friend for lunch, I wait at the entrance to the restaurant. I sit and watch for her until she arrives. I don't want to miss her.

CONNECTING THE DOTS

Stay alert and watch for God to reveal His presence.

How many times have we missed seeing God? We carve out time to meet Him but fail to watch for His arrival. We call to Him but move on with our day when no immediate answer comes. We kill time pouring over a menu of options, deciding what *we* wanted to accomplish or running absent-mindedly through a myriad of tasks.

Our distracted focus both deafens and blinds us from noticing God's presence. We miss Him, letting poles of self-reliance block our view. Or impatience propels us toward the door. We miss seeing Him even though He is there.

When exiled from Egypt and while herding his father-in-law's sheep through the desert, Moses saw a burning bush not consumed by the fire. God called to him from the bush, but only *AFTER* Moses took note of the bush *AND* turned aside from his sheepherding to see what was going on. Only then did Moses hear God speak (Exodus 3:4-5).

The poet, Elizabeth Barrett Browning, once wrote:

Earth's crammed with heaven
and every common bush afire with God.
But only he who sees takes off his shoes;
the rest sit around and pluck blackberries.[15]

God reveals Himself every day. But He does not always come through the obvious, the front door. He might show up in the common, ordinary bushes afire with His presence. Or He may disclose Himself through His hand-shaping circumstances, orchestrating timely coincidences, or placing people in our path just when we need them, or they need us. Or He may simply utter our name.

However the Lord arrives, if we stay alert and watch for Him, He promises we will find Him (Jeremiah 29:13). So, …

Keep your eyes open for God, watch for his
works; be alert for signs of his presence.
Psalm 105:4 (The Message)

SECTION 6

CHOICES

51

BUILD ON THE RIGHT
FOUNDATION

· · · · · · · ● ● ● ● ● ● ● ● ● · · · · ·

I never traveled to see Italy and its medieval structures but find the Tower of Pisa fascinating. In 1173 the Italian architect Bonnano Pisano began work on what would become his most famous project: An eight-story, 185-foot-tall bell tower for the Cathedral of the city of Pisa.

After constructing three stories, builders discovered one teensy little problem...softer soil than anticipated and a foundation too shallow to hold the structure. Sure enough, the whole structure began to tilt...and tilt some more.

During the 176 years in which the Tower of Pisa was under construction, the architect and builders attempted to compensate for the tilt. They shored up the foundation and built new stories slightly taller on the shorter side to make the tower look straight. Later, the heavier of its seven bells were silenced, believing that their movement worsened the tower's lean. But nothing worked. Nothing made the Leaning Tower of Pisa straight again.

The tower has stood for over 800 years, but it leans 18 feet away from where it should be (10 degrees from the vertical according to engineers). Experts predict the Tower of Pisa will fall into a heap of rubble one day because it wasn't built on the right foundation.

CONNECTING THE DOTS

Choose to build your life on the rock-solid foundation of Jesus Christ rather than the soft shifting sands of self-determination.

Construct a life founded on the Word of God, as best exemplified by His Son. Instead of lashing out in anger, speak in love. Instead of sowing discord, build unity. Instead of striking dissention, strike harmony.

Then when inevitable storms come and winds blow, we will not falter or fall into a heap of rubble. We will weather them, resting in assurance that God is with us and never leaves us. This truth holds for individuals, cities, and nations alike.

Everyone then who hears these words of mine and acts on them
will be like a wise man who built his house on rock. The rain
fell, the floods came, and the winds flew and beat on that house,
but it did not fall, because it had been founded on rock.
Matthew 7:24-25 (NRSV)

52

COME AS YOU ARE

· · · · · · · · ● ◉ ● · · · · · · · · ·

"You look lovely the way you are. Let's go," my husband coaxed me toward the door. Was that a compliment or him hurrying me to leave?

Jim's last-minute suggestion of lunch at the Cotton Patch restaurant made my mouth water thinking about a double order of their fried okra and homemade biscuits. The problem...I wasn't dressed for going out in public. The granny jeans and plain t-shirt I wore were at the top of our daughter's "What Not to Wear" list. Worse yet was my no-make-up look.

The last time I poked my nose out of the house sans full face of foundation, eyeliner, and mascara, I was twelve years old. On that Saturday morning, the doorbell rang at 7 a.m. While still shaking cobwebs out of my brain, I thumped through the living room in rumpled pajamas and pink fluffy slippers to see who came calling at the crack of dawn.

"Surprise!" my friend stood outside our screened door with her mother. "It's a 'Come as You Are' party. C'mon!"

I wiped sleep out of my eyes and ran fingers through my haystack of hair flying in every direction. I hardly looked presentable to go anywhere, much less a party. Mom snuck up behind me and pushed me out the door, chuckling, "Have a great time."

"No way." I mumbled while putting on a mask of joviality to hide my self-consciousness. Just like I now did with my husband. Too weary to argue and hearing the cry of fried okra beckoning from the Cotton Patch stovetop, I relented and strolled to the car. Sans makeup. In frumpy jeans.

My moment of truth arrived. Seated at the restaurant, the waitress asked for our order. Lowering the menu, I used to hide my face, I looked the lady straight in the eye. "I'll have two fried okras, green beans and roast beef."

"Good choice," she responded, returning my eye contact with a genuine smile and approving nod. No startled look or cringe at the sight of my freshly scrubbed face. Well, this was going better than expected. Even fellow diners didn't faint or point at my shiny nose and whisper.

With new-found confidence, I vowed to try the clean look more often and remembered that "Come as You Are" party. I arrived to find eight other girlfriends, all in various stages of dishevelment. No one cared how I looked. They welcomed me just as I was.

CONNECTING THE DOTS

God calls to us, "Just come as you are." Choose to go to Him. To accept Christ as our Savior and Lord of our life.

He welcomes us, despite wrinkles and disheveled state, weariness, messes, hurts, faults, or fears. That's grace. Christ's sacrifice on the cross cleaned us up already. He made us presentable to approach God, our Father and Creator, as His beloved child. The Lord invites us to come, sit, and talk awhile. He calls us to come, get to know Him, and pour out our hearts to Him, just as we are.

Even before he made the world, God loved us and
chose us in Christ to be holy and without fault in his eyes.
God decided in advance to adopt us into his own family
by bringing us to himself through Jesus Christ.
This is what he wanted to do,
and it gave him great pleasure.
So, we praise God for the glorious grace
he has poured out on us who belong to his dear Son.
Ephesians 1:4-6 (NLT)

53

HERE I AM

· · · · · · · ● ◉ ● · · · · · · · ·

As a mom, I enjoyed a good game of hide-and-seek. Especially when I wanted to be left alone. I hid in the bathroom and locked the door. Sinking into a warm bubble bath with waters up to my chin, I closed my eyes and tuned out the world. For about 2 minutes before...

Tap, tap, tap. Tap, tap, tap.

Maybe if I'm quiet, they'll go away. Just give me ten more minutes.

Tap, tap, tap. "Mommy? Mommy, I want you," my three-year-old daughter's voice pleaded from the other side of the door. Deep inhale, slow exhale. Stand up, grab a towel to wrap around my bubbled body, and open the door.

"Okay, Jessica. Let's play hide and seek. You found me. Now you hide and I'll seek." She flashed me her impish grin before turning to patter down the hallway and into her room.

I counted aloud to ten, then warned her, "Ready or not, here..."

Before I could finish and duck back into my waiting bubble bath, Jessica darted out of her hiding place and raced towards me. She lunged at my legs, wrapped her arms around my knees, and giggled, "Here I am, Mommy."

I wasn't always as willing as my daughter to be found…or found out. Lack of confidence or fear of judgment held me behind a façade of poise and self-assurance.

For instance, my vacation approached a month after our hide-and-seek game. People asked how I planned to spend my days off from the corporate hustle. Initially I hid behind a vague response - catching up on chores, taking a short trip, and reading. Not totally misleading.

I was doing it again. Hiding. The real me hid from public scrutiny. Felt insignificant and afraid to tell the truth. To say out loud how God prompted me to use this vacation. After all, what if they judged me? Or what if I heard wrong? Or failed?

But, taking a page out of the lesson primer of my child, who couldn't wait to be found, I came out of hiding. Running to the Father's promised faithfulness, I shared my plan to attend the Christian Communicators Conference. To develop the speaker and teacher in me. Rather than hide from the truth, I declared, "Here I am."

CONNECTING THE DOTS

Choose to come out of hiding. Instead of running away *from* God and His call, run *to* Him. Rather than hiding behind busyness, distractions, tiredness, denial, fear, or whatever, declare instead, "Here I am."

The Apostle Paul frequently urged us to "…fearlessly make known the mystery of the gospel" (Ephesians 6:19-20, NIV). God did not put us here to play hide and seek. Not with Him (like Adam and Eve) nor with those He places in our path (like Jonah with Ninevah). Rather, He put out a casting call. Everyone who chooses to answer gets a part in His unfolding story. Sometimes we get the lead. More often we will play supporting roles, have walk-on parts, or fill a behind-the-scenes role. Either way, He cast us in the perfect part for His purposes at a moment or season in time.

Granted, the Lord's call does not always come at times most convenient to schedules, dispositions, or reputations we built for the eyes of others. However, when His call comes, choose to come out of hiding and declare boldly...

Then I heard the voice of the LORD saying, "Whom shall I send?
And who will go for us?" And I said, "Here am I. Send me!"
Isaiah 6:8 (NIV)

54

OBEY THE LIFEGUARD

What a demanding week. Between triple digit temperatures wilting energy, gardens frying in the drought, and the debt debate churning fear about the economy, who isn't ready for a break from daily burdens? That's why I envied the neighbor's two sons splashing with abandon in their pool while Dad watched from his deck beneath the shade of a large umbrella.

I envied that simpler time in life. I wanted to be ten years old again. During that summer, Mom let me walk six blocks to join other kids for a swim in the neighborhood pool. She sent me off with only one warning, "Obey the lifeguard." Usually he was a tanned and muscled college jock who sat atop his tall chair for a birds-eye view of the pool and young swimmers.

The pool opened at 11:00 a.m. Fifty kids waited for the lifeguard to unlock the gate and motion us in. Once we found a place for our towels and flip-flops along the ten-foot cyclone fence lining the pool, he blew his whistle. We stood at attention while he reviewed the rules.

"Walk, don't run, on the slick pavement, no diving into the shallow end, and no horseplay like jumping off someone's shoulders onto another swimmer. Got it?" His gaze circled the fence to catch the eyes of every child nodding agreement.

"Now, pair up with a buddy." I grabbed my friend's hand. "When you hear three short blasts from my whistle, clear the pool and stand with your buddy. We'll number off to be sure everyone is accounted for."

With that, the lifeguard blew his whistle, and fifty pairs of legs raced to jump into the waiting water. During the next two hours, amid splashing, shrill giggles and cannonballs off the diving board, I heard an occasional tweet of the lifeguard's whistle as he pointed to rule breakers, "Slow down...No shoving...Stop clowning around."

"Hey, quit that." The dad next door broke into my memory. He stood at the edge of his pool, without a whistle but pointing to his oldest son. "Stop roughhousing. You'll hurt your brother," he demanded. Just like my neighborhood lifeguard reminded us when we were doing something hurtful to ourselves or others. Just like the Father reminds His children.

CONNECTING THE DOTS

The Lord is our eternal lifeguard. Choose to listen to and obey whatever He says. Even during times when evil has the upper hand on our world.

God left us His Word to guide us in how best to live. He gave His only Son to redeem us from our sinful nature. He sent us a "buddy," His Holy Spirit, to point us in the right direction and warn us when we are about to harm ourselves or others. We can enjoy an abundant life if we link arms with His Holy Spirit daily.

In our enthusiasm to enjoy life, we must avoid getting sucked into "clowning around" or shoving "what's right" aside for our self-interests. Our Lord Lifeguard goes before us to prepare the way, protect us as we travel through challenging times, and guards the rear as we march toward eternity with Him. Our Father wants no one to perish (2 Peter 3:9) but to ensure all His children are accounted for and arrive safely at our heavenly home.

Knowing this, feel free to jump into life's pool and swim with abandon.

> *"If you'll hold on to me for dear life," says GOD," I'll get you out of any trouble. I'll give you the best of care if you'll only get to know and trust me. Call me and I'll answer, be at your side in bad times; I'll rescue you, then throw you a party. I'll give you a long life, give you a long drink of salvation!*
> Psalm 91:14-16 (The Message)

55

MAKE ROOM FOR THE LIGHT

· · · · · · · · · ● · · · · · · · · · · ·

"Gross. Isn't this clean enough? It's icky." The six-year-old child's wavy blond hair fell around her face as she peered into the hole carved into the top of the pumpkin. "Well, is it?" she whined to her nine-year-old brother, who kneeled close by and bent over his own pumpkin with both hands thrust inside.

Remembering my past pumpkin carving rituals, I paused in the middle of sorting pansies to see if someone would rescue the child and finish the task for her.

"Not clean enough," the brother declared after examining his sister's pumpkin. The girl rolled her eyes, sat back on her heels and sighed, tossing her scoop to the ground. She folded her arms over her chest and thrust out her lower lip. Her brother shrugged his shoulders and returned to his own pumpkin prep. She'd get no help from him.

The girl's mom paused from leaf raking and glanced toward her children.

Ahh, mom to the rescue, I assumed. Wrong.

Mom leaned on her rake where she stopped her yard work. She encouraged her daughter to continue. "Scrape it clean. You must get out *all* the seeds and stringy stuff."

"Why?" the child still resisted the disgusting task.

"So you can put the candle inside and let the light shine through."

The young girl cocked her head, as if considering whether she wanted a light in her pumpkin. After sixty seconds of weighing options, her wrinkled forehead relaxed. She picked up her scoop and kneeled to finish cleaning the pumpkin's icky insides.

"Now I'm done," the child's voice drifted with the breeze into my yard. I watched the father round the corner from back of the house and walk over to the newspaper full of pumpkin goo. He inspected his daughter's work, nodded, and smiled as if to say, "Well done." Then, without a word, he lowered himself to the ground and began to carve the pumpkin's face through which the light would shine.

CONNECTING THE DOTS

Like my young neighbor, choose to scoop out sinful habits or thoughts. Make room for the light of Christ to come into and shine through our life.

We all sin and fall short of God's glory (Romans 3:23-24). We all contain goo – those yucky habits and thoughts that grow within us so naturally. Until we empty ourselves of the goo, God cannot carve and shape our hearts and life into the full potential through which His light can shine.

If we ask, God freely forgives us. But we must ask. Our Father will not force His will upon us. And, no one can ask for us on our behalf. We must do it for ourselves. Once we ask and allow the mystery of the cross to empty us of sin, our Father will round the corner of our life and declare, "Well done." He will make us a new creation through which the light of His Holy Spirit can shine to reflect His image to all the world.

> *... let us throw off everything that hinders and the sin that so easily entangles. And let us run with perseverance the race marked out for us, fixing our eyes on Jesus, the pioneer and perfecter of faith.*
> Hebrews 12:1-2 (NIV)

56

LOST AND FOUND

· · · · · · · · ● ● ● ● ● ● ● ● ● ● · · · · · ·

"Uh-oh, where are they? Daddy? Mommy?" Twisting my skinny, six-year-old body around to look back down the shoreline, I peered at the footprints scrambled in the sand. I squinted to see if I could pick out the ones that were mine and would point me back to my family's beach blanket. No, they all looked alike.

I shaded my eyes against the noonday sun and looked up, hoping to spot a familiar adult face. I didn't. Lost, the only thing in front of me was a forest of big people legs.

Panic lapped at my feet like the wave that crashed onto the shore and crept inland, overtaking my toes. Then it receded back towards the ocean, pulling with it my self-confidence – the same certainty that had pushed me in my prissy red-flowered swimsuit and bathing cap into thinking I was big enough to explore alone.

The towel I carried like a princess cape winged out from either side of my back now drooped about my shoulders. They slumped forward as prickles of fear inched up my spine.

I searched up and down the beach for my mother's white swimsuit with the single teardrop pearl adorning the front. Nothing. I looked for my dad's sky blue trunks and the cowgirl tattooed on his leg. I couldn't find her winking at me from the side of his calf.

I retraced my path. Still no sight of mommy, daddy or the passel of relatives who came with us to the beach. Only a sea of laughing and sunbathing strangers crowded around me. I turned again and headed the other direction, frantically scanning the crowds for family. *Where are they?*

I screamed into the breeze when he yanked my arm and whirled me around.

"Daddy." I grabbed his leg and squeezed tightly, not even caring he swatted my bottom for wandering away. All that mattered was he found me.

Daddy forgave me and still loved me despite my disobedience to stay within his sights. I knew this because I saw the relief in his moist eyes. Hand-in-hand we walked back to the family blanket.

CONNECTING THE DOTS

Choose to repent whenever and as soon as we discover we've wandered from the Lord.

The Hebrew word for "repent" is *shuv*. Literally, it means to head back by the road from which we came and return by the right one. When we stray, our Father looks for us. He eagerly watches for sight of our return. And, when we do, He is there, ready to forgive and welcome us back.

Our Father never stops loving us, despite our wandering from His Word. Our God is the same father who watched for his young son, who left home and squandered both his life and money. The young man finally came to his senses and decided to return home. Even while he was a long distance from home, when the father spotted him, he...

...was filled with compassion for him; he ran to his
son, threw his arms around him and kissed him.
Luke 15:20 (NIV)

He loved his Son...and loves each of us...that much.

57

DIG INTO LIFE

· · · · · · · · ●● ● ●● · · · · · · · ·

I first heard about the Dead Sea Scrolls in my religion classes in college. Like a six-year-old dancing before the family tree of unopened gifts on Christmas morning, I looked forward to seeing on exhibit the oldest known manuscripts of the Book that changed the world.

Walking through the limestone archway entrance, I traveled back in time. Life-sized pictures of the Qumran caves beamed me to the desolate mountainside that protected the scrolls for over 2,000 years until a shepherd boy discovered them while looking for his lost goat. My fingertips rested within an inch of the sacred documents held within environmentally controlled plexiglass cases.

I pictured the Essene scribe, hunched over a table with only an oil lamp to light his work. He dipped his pen into a tiny bowl of ink made from iron salts and tree fungus. With painstaking accuracy, he copied the biblical text onto the goatskin parchment, his script only a quarter inch high. How long did it take him to copy the books of Moses, the Psalms, or Isaiah?

The tour ended, but my husband humored me to keep the experience going. We walked outside and strolled one block to the green tent that sheltered a simulated Qumran archaeological dig site. I looked forward to troweling through sand to uncover my souvenir, a 2,000-year-old potsherd…

Until the tour guide killed the moment. At the end of his lecture, he said, "I'm happy to answer questions. And we've hidden over 20,000 pieces of broken pottery from Qumran for the children to dig if they want."

For the children? Hey, I came to dig. Can't I dig? The website promised, "The Qumran Simulated Dig Site lets visitors of *all* ages experience what it's like to be a real archaeologist."

Five kids grabbed trowels and headed to the designated area. We adults stayed planted where we stood. I walked away without yielding to the child-like thrill of uncovering pieces of the ancient Middle East where Jesus walked.

Regret. But I can't blame the doctoral student. *I* let his words and assumptions stop me. *I* couldn't let go of the "stuffy adult" tapes in my head. The ones that said, *you'll look silly. You're too old for this.* I let adult rules rule. I acted the Pharisee, all educated and too sophisticated to let the child in me experience a kingdom moment.

On my way out, I reached down and grabbed a crumb of Qumran pottery lying at my feet. I vowed to visit the exhibit again. But next time — and praise God who gives "next times" — I would go with the mindset of a child – humble, curious, and open to whatever God wants me to uncover. Next time, I would dig into life with gusto.

Connecting the Dots

Choose to live life with child-like humility.

Give up so much self-consciousness. Stop worrying about how our actions will add or take away from status attained or recognition for our efforts. Go ahead. Dig into life with curiosity and a sense of adventure. Experience what God wants to show or give us. Jesus Himself warned us of the pitfall of not doing so when He said,

Truly I tell you, unless you change and become like little children, you will never enter the kingdom of heaven. Therefore, whoever takes the lowly position of this child is the greatest in the kingdom of heaven.
Matthew 18:3-4 (NIV)

58

TAKE THE PLUNGE; THROW YOUR WHOLE SELF INTO IT

· · · · · · ● ● ● ◉ ● ● ● ● · · · · · ·

I shivered as the breeze off the bay water whipped through my light jacket. I hadn't expected San Francisco's spring weather to start the day with such cool mornings. As a cold-natured, Texas gal whose fingernails were turning blue and lips quivering, I was downright freezing as Jim and I walked along the quiet shore, enjoying the first day of our vacation.

"You could be colder," Jim teased. "Like those guys." I followed his finger pointing to a group of people huddled on the pier that jutted over the water. They wore only tights, tank tops, and ... what was that on their heads? Swim caps?

Surely, they are not.... The thought hardly registered in my frozen brain when someone in the group blew a whistle. The entire tangle of barely covered bodies plunged into the bay. The polar bear swim club was in session.

No toe-testing the frigid waves first. No wading or slowly lowering one's body to become accustomed to icy water. They just threw their whole selves into the bay and swam.

CONNECTING THE DOTS

When God calls us to an assignment, take the plunge. Choose to throw your whole self into it.

The polar bear club reminded me how best to approach the tidal wave of challenges that came my way. In some instances, I watched from the sidelines, not ready to commit. In others, I waded into the waters only to my knees. With arms crossed and holding my sides, I pondered whether to venture any further. Doubt in my abilities, uncertainty about my survival, and wariness about whether God would or could deliver me through the ordeal this time, all held me from fully submerging in the waters.

Then, one day the Apostle Paul's words to the Corinthians grabbed me by the shoulders, looked me in the eye, and said,

> *... in a single victorious stroke of Life, all three – sin, guilt, and death – are gone, the gift of our Master, Jesus Christ. Thank God. With all this going for us, ... don't hold back. Throw yourselves into the work of the Master, confident that nothing you do for him is a waste of time and effort.*
> 1 Corinthians 15:58 (The Message)

That is what Christ's life, death and resurrection bought for me, for us. So, when God calls us to an assignment that seems too big to handle, take the plunge. Trust God and join His polar bear swim club in session.

59

NAMING YOUR DREAM

When Mom dropped me off for Career Day in seventh grade, I walked into the school full of possibilities. I could choose to be anything I wanted. Mom said so, and Dad agreed.

I chose "engineer." *Maybe an architectural engineer.* Mentally, I fingered Dad's mechanical drawing set. With the reverence given to a surgeon's sterile tray of instruments before delicate surgery, I unsnapped the case. Inside, on a soft, sapphire blue felt holder, lay a steel protractor, a 6" ruler, and mechanical compasses for drawing perfect circles and arcs.

To use these in a job would be divine. *Yes, engineer. I like that possibility.*

"Kids," my math teacher's booming voice startled me back to the classroom. From his perch on a stool in front of the room, he warned, "When you choose vocations to explore today, make sure they're appropriate. For instance, if you're a girl, you may not want to choose engineering."

I slunk in my chair, mortified. With eyes darting side to side to ensure no one saw my selection sheet, I covered my dream and erased the check mark by engineering. No one had told me being a girl limited my career choices.

Elizabeth and Zechariah faced the same dilemma. They dreamed of having a child. But none came. Elizabeth remained barren until well into her senior years. An angel then appeared to Zechariah and proclaimed their dream was about to come true. "Your wife Elizabeth will bear you a son, and you will name him John" (Luke 1:13, NIV).

After Elizabeth bore her son, well-meaning neighbors and kin gasped in horror when she bucked Jewish tradition by giving her child a name different from his father's or anyone else in their family tree.

But Elizabeth and Zechariah stood firm. They refused to name their son anything other than John … the name the angel of the Lord declared their dream should be called. The dream that had filled their hearts into old age and well beyond Elizabeth's child-bearing years (Luke 1:57-66).

I now tuck Dad's mechanical drawing set in my center desk drawer and pull it out occasionally. Not to mourn what could have been, for my dream of an engineering career faded as new dreams took shape.

Instead, that mechanical drawing reminds me to celebrate what I learned on seventh grade Career Day. To resist allowing anyone to rename the dreams I dream...the ones God puts on my heart. Because I want to be what *He* created me to be. Mom said so. And my Father agreed.

CONNECTING THE DOTS

God plants His desires in our hearts. When we commit to Him, His desires become ours. Choose to *never* let anyone rename the desires and dreams God names in you.

Be aware, those dreams and desires may not fit the stereotype, typical norm, or expectations of another. Yet, if they are righteous and ones in which time passes without our awareness, then they are probably the dreams and desires God is using to fulfill all He wants us to be and do for His glory. Pursue with dogged determination those dreams and desires.

Take delight in the LORD, and
he will give you the desires of your heart.
Commit your way to the LORD;
trust in him and he will do this:
He will make your righteous reward shine like the dawn,
your vindication like the noonday sun.
Psalm 37:4-6 (NIV)

60

PLANNING: WHERE TO?

My family vacations started nothing like my friend's. Her dad piled wife, kids, and family pets into the car. He then drove to the end of the block where he stopped, turned to his family, and asked, "So, where to this time?"

Say what? No plan in place? No reservations? No destination researched and plotted with every rest stop between here and there? Hand me the brown paper bag to breathe into because just hearing my friend's version of a family trip makes me hyperventilate. How could they not plan in advance?

Like I do, especially when traveling unfamiliar territory. I'm armed with my GPS (Global Positioning System for navigational tracking), a print-out of MapQuest's route to my destination, and my husband's directions scribbled on a scratch pad. With all three, and thirty spare minutes built in for getting lost, I should arrive.

The plan works perfectly … until it doesn't. What should I do when the GPS points me to an exit different from hubby's directions? Or road construction detours me through streets not mentioned in any of my plans? Or I somehow miss the next turn?

My life plan can unfold that way, too. I hold my end goal in mind and a bullet-proof plan to get there. Yet, the process doesn't always go as outlined. Others' plans or actions thwart mine. The unexpected swerves into my lane and sideswipes me. Circumstances block the path I chose.

Planning has its place, but so does flexibility. Take the Israelites' exodus from Egypt, for example. They traveled like my friend. After they packed up, crossed the Red Sea, and left slavery behind, they asked, "Where to?"

God answered, "The land I will show you." The Israelites traveled by a cloud-GPS; the one God provided. They never knew where they headed except to the land He promised. They knew only that His cloud led the way.

When and wherever it stopped, the Hebrew people stopped. If the cloud stayed, they stayed. When the cloud moved, they moved. Oh, they grumbled along the way because they couldn't see how things would turn out. (I'm certain I would have been among those who groused.) Yet, they chose to let the cloud guide them.

Last week, I prayed, "Lord, where to now?" This morning, He answered, "Just follow My cloud."

For me God speaks through various clouds. He speaks through the cloud of peace that settles in my heart when I am where I need to be and stay, even when circumstances are difficult. Sometimes, it's the cloud of nagging restlessness or dissatisfaction that hums through my soul without good reason and says it's time to move even though life is easy and I'm happy where I am. Other times it's a random thought, the passion that swells in my heart, or a nudge to my spirit pointing me in the direction I need to go.

But what about our planning? It has its place when traveling to a God-given destination. But God's plan and process trump mine.

CONNECTING THE DOTS
• •

Choose to put personal planning in its place – behind the Lord's cloud. Move forward boldly to the "land" He shows us, yet with our faith-filled *tentative* plan.

Hold personal plans loosely, and always follow the Lord's cloud. Trust His plan and process above ours. Move whenever and wherever God's cloud moves. He won't always give us the GPS or MapQuest detailed instructions to the destination. Nor does He scribble directions on a scratch pad. Instead, He simply says, "Follow My cloud."

*When the cloud moved from its place over the Tent, the Israelites
moved, and wherever the cloud stopped, the Israelites camped
... Sometimes the cloud stayed over the Tent for a long time, but
the Israelites obeyed the Lord and did not move. At the Lord's
command the people camped, and at his command they moved.*
Numbers 9: 17-20 (NCV)

SECTION 7

AGING TO PERFECTION

61

LESSONS GONE VIRAL: REFLECT, RESET, AND REALIGN

· · · · · · · · · ● · · · · · · · · · · ·

Within three months of the corona virus hitting China, it spread westward to Japan, Korea, and Italy, and across oceans to the United States. In March President Trump called for social distancing, closing restaurants, and canceling events with more than ten people. He hoped our nation could ease these restrictions by Easter.

But here we are, five months later and counting. Hopes for instant gratification dashed against the rocks of realities. Two weeks of sheltering in place had yet to flatten the statistical curve of diagnosed cases.

Economists predict 18-24 months or more before we recover from the virus' social and economic impact. Yet, even with recovery, the lengthy epidemic has transformed us. The same two catch phrases that now likely shape consumerism can also shape and guide our faith and spiritual decisions: prepare and protect.

Will this service or product prepare me for the future? For many of us, enforced quarantine and its accompanying shortages and losses refocused priorities. The question for the future: What essentials must I have and keep in supply? What poor habits and attitudes will

I shed going forward? Which ones do I keep or attain that better prepare me for the future? Which ones deepen my relationship with Christ, advance His kingdom on earth, and bring glory to His name?

Will this service or product protect me? Again, where will I invest time and effort in what arms me to fight the enemy and his temptations and deceit designed to separate me from the Lord? Will I face each day by putting on the belt of truth, the breastplate of righteousness, the shoes of peace, the helmet of salvation, the shield of faith, and the sword of the Spirit, which is the Word of God?

The corona virus hit the pause/reset button in more ways than one. Ironically, the outbreak came in the middle of Lent – a time to repent. Time to reflect, reset, and realign my life to a new normal. One that follows more closely the example of Jesus who surrendered his whole being to the Father.

CONNECTING THE DOTS

When a life-changing season comes – like COVID-19, financial crisis, health concerns, or breaks in relationships – avoid hitting a snooze button and going back to sleep in old habits and attitudes. Avoid blindly stabbing at buttons to shut off the sounded alarms. Instead, reflect and learn the right lessons and "unlearn" the wrong ones. Instead, re-awaken, reset, and realign our lives to God's call upon us.

J. D. Walt, founder of Seedbed, wrote, "Everything that happens is not God's will, but God has a will in everything that happens."[1]

Even when life gets harder before it gets easier during these wilderness-like seasons, we can trust the Lord is orchestrating our circumstances to prepare and protect us, perhaps beyond what we see or can know. We can lean into letting Him shape and mold us anew – physically, economically, socially, emotionally, and spiritually. Epidemics and pandemics can be a time in which God further prepares and effectively uses us to advance His kingdom. If we let Him.

> *But God is doing what is best for us, training us to live God's holy best. At the time, discipline isn't much fun. It always feels like it's going against the grain. Later, of course, it pays off handsomely, for it's the well-trained who find themselves mature in their relationship with God.*
> Hebrews 12:11 (The Message)

62

WHICH IS BETTER: MORE OR LESS?

• • • • • • • • • ● • • • • • • • • •

"Who thinks more is better than less?" An adult posed that question in one of my favorite commercials. The kindergartner explains without hesitation, "More! We want more."

I can relate. Being an ambitious oldest or perhaps just a product of society, I often wanted more...more friends, more house, more clothes, more status, more responsibility, etc. More was an indicator of success. More brought happiness, at least temporarily.

As the years fly by, though, I lose more and get less. I am ...

> ... less of a targeted consumer for market groups.
> ... less desirable as a patient to doctors. (Like the one who turned me away because of my age...and I wasn't even on Medicare yet.)
> ... less apt to succeed at becoming President of anything.
> ... less likely to be considered a future up-and-comer.
> ... less capable of keeping up with Billy's Boot Camp workout video.

… less time with my daughter who is now married with two children to tend.

… less of others'-imposed priorities and agendas defining my day.

However, I soon realize that as I give in to the flow of getting *less*, I wind up having *more...*

… more time to read and reflect on God's Word.

… more free time to read a magazine or curl up on the couch with a good romance or mystery novel.

… more time available for lunch dates or an afternoon of Canasta with friends.

… more flexibility to engage in what I feel passionate about.

… more focus on the needs of others.

… more openness to surprises and new experiences.

… more quiet time to deepen my relationship with God.

Which is better? More or less? I regret I took so long to discover the best answer. When it's less about me, there can be more of Christ in me. As I become less self-centered, I can become more Christ-centered.

As I am less consumed with my desires, dreams, and agendas, I am more capable of tuning in to where God is at work around me. And the more I glimpse my God at work, the better I understand His assignments for me with the unique combination of strengths and gifts He put in me.

Which is better, more or less? I used to choose more. Now I choose less. So that I wind up with more of that which truly sustains my soul and being.

CONNECTING THE DOTS

Choose to become less so that Christ in us can become more. Choose to put self in the background so Christ can come into the foreground.

This is the assigned moment for him to move into
the center, while I slip off to the sidelines.
John 3:30 (The Message)

63

CALLED BY THE
HOUND OF HEAVEN

· · · · · · · · · ● ● ● ● · · · · · · · ·

The minister's words gushed out of her mouth. "I *reeeeeeally* need Disciple 1 teachers," she pleaded, "Will you lead that class?"

My heart pushed me to say *Yes*. My mind screamed *No*.

Three months earlier, a Bible study teacher suggested the idea. "You have the spiritual gift for teaching. You should lead a Disciple class next fall."

I resisted. I cringed, remembering the Spiritual Gifts inventory[2] I completed for his class. One hundred and sixty questions later, I tallied results to discover my gift.

Teaching.

Unnerving experiences while student teaching during college danced in my memory. *That can't be right. I answered some questions wrong.* So, I did what any good Christian did in moments of doubt… or resistance. I prayed and retook the test.

The result? Teaching again.

Okay, third time's the charm. I retook it three days later. Teaching tallied #1. By a decent margin. That left me no choice but to remind God, and my Bible study teacher, why this was *not* their best idea. (You may recognize reasons used yourself in daunting situations) ...

... "I'm not trained in the Bible."

... "Just the thought of presenting in front of others puts me in a faint."

... "I'm short on energy and time to prepare weekly lessons."

Summer months with no classes offered me reprieve from the gnawing feeling that God called me. That's why I felt safe testing God's intentions that autumn Sunday morning. The urgent request, "Disciple Teachers Needed," caught my eye in the church newsletter.

"Lord," I prayed, "if you want me to lead a Disciple Bible study, then give me a clear sign. Like with Gideon. Prove your will for me."

His answer came within two hours.

After encouraging our Sunday school class to attend a Disciple study if they had not yet done so, two ladies approached me with questions. The last one stunned me to silence, "Gloria, will you consider teaching Disciple 1?"

The morning's tossed fleece darted across my mind. *That's the last class I would consider teaching.* Feeling my resolve weaken, I mumbled an evasive answer and hurried off to join my husband in the sanctuary.

An hour later and upon leaving the worship service, I spotted our new education minister — the one who posted the need for Disciple teachers. She stood alone in the lobby.

I paused at the exit. *Surely, if I wait long enough, others will command her attention to get acquainted.*

Not one of several hundred exiting parishioners approached the minister. She remained planted in her spot, looking around as everyone streamed past. Unexpectedly, the milling people parted like the Red Sea, making a clear path between her and me.

All right stop hounding me. I'll introduce myself. I extended my hand to welcome her. Before I could grab the words and tuck them back into my mouth, I heard my voice utter, "I'll teach Disciple 1 if you need someone."

My next thought attached a silent disclaimer, *Anything but Disciple 1 — too much reading. Way past my capability.*

The new minister clutched my hand in between hers and replied, "You're an answer to my prayers. I really need a Disciple 1 teacher."

CONNECTING THE DOTS

Our Lord is the Hound of Heaven. Even if we try to hide, He tracks us down. He loves and wants us to be in relationship with Him that much.

And, do we think for a moment the Lord would call us to a divine assignment and then allow us to fail? Never. He arms us with a unique combination of gifts, talents, and resources to do what He calls us to do. Lead with those.

Before a word is on my tongue you, LORD, know it completely. You hem me in behind and before, and you lay your hand upon me. Such knowledge is too wonderful for me, too lofty for me to attain. Where can I go from your Spirit? Where can I flee from your presence?
Psalm 139:4-7 (NIV)

64

GO IN THE STRENGTHS YOU HAVE AND DO WHATEVER HE TELLS YOU

· · · · · · · · ● ● ● ● ● ● ● ● ● · · · ·

While my heart pushed me to say *Yes* to teaching a nine-month Bible study, my mind still screamed *No*. How did I get to this point? From the toss of a Gideon-like fleece to standing in the sanctuary with an associate minister, who threw her arms around me and blessed me for volunteering to teach what I never intended to volunteer for?

Maybe God led me to this moment. Still, I feared failure. That pushed me to follow Gideon's lead and toss a second fleece. *Forgive me, Lord, for asking again, but if you intend for me to teach this study, then enroll a full class — twelve students.*

Only four signed up during the next two weeks. *Aha. I knew You didn't want me to teach.* I dodged that bullet, until orientation night. Twenty-four showed up for class.

I relented. God must be calling me. Though I still doubted my credentials and abilities for such a daunting task. Until a few days later when the Bible story of the wedding at Cana gave me the answer.

The host ran out of wine, and servants were probably in a dither about what to do to avoid public embarrassment. Mary spoke to her son, Jesus, about the problem. When he rebuffed her concern and offered no solution, Mary was not deterred. She turned to the servants and said, "Do whatever he [Jesus] tells you" (John 2:5, NRSV).

They did, and he did, and water became fine wine.

In my own dither to pull together two hours of material week after week, I did what the Holy Spirit told me. I read the participant and leader guides, researched where I lacked background or details, and outlined how best to approach each session.

When I stood before 24 students in class, Mary's refrain played in my mind, "Do whatever He tells you." Night after night, the Spirit took over where I fell short. He prompted flashes of insight to answer a student's question – insights not in my preparatory notes and that I never knew before. Together we searched for meaning in "throw away" verses[4] I initially passed over. Brief outlines exploded to fill two hours of discussion. Student "aha's" resounded when I feared none existed.

CONNECTING THE DOTS

To turn watery assignments into wine, ask for God's help and do whatever the Holy Spirit says.

Gideon's mind screamed "no" too. He gave plenty of excuses when God called him to be a judge and deliver the Israelites from their oppressor. But he did what the Lord told him. Gideon even pared down his army from 32,000 and fought to victory with only 300 men against a Midianite army "as thick as locusts" and 135,000 strong (Judges 7:12 NRSV).

The Lord never calls us to an assignment and then allows us to fail. Like Gideon, we can go in the strengths we have and do what He tells us. Why? He gives us a secret weapon – the Holy Spirit – who dwells within us and goes with us the moment we accept Christ. (See John 14:16-17; 2 Corinthians 1:22; 2 Corinthians 6:16; 1 John 4:3.) His Spirit empowers us supernaturally for divinely appointed tasks. He equips, transforms, and connects the dots for us to minister however God calls us.

God's assignments require only that we go in the strength we have and do whatever His Spirit tells us at that moment. It is enough. Where we are "less," He adds the "more."

> *When the angel of the LORD appeared to Gideon, he*
> *said, "The LORD is with you, mighty warrior."*
> *… The LORD turned to him and said, "Go in the strength you have*
> *and save Israel out of Midian's hand. Am I not sending you?"*
> Judges 6:12,14 (NIV)

65

WHAT I HAVE, I GIVE YOU...

Trained as a social worker, what was I doing working in a financial organization? After ten years with a hospital, restlessness sent me in search of a new opportunity. Through the most unlikely avenue – a newspaper ad – I landed a job in the most unlikely place.

What value could I bring to the world of investments, markets and bottom-line margins? Everyone at the company sported financial backgrounds but me. Mine was limited to balancing the family budget. I barely passed Economics 101 and never traded a stock or bond.

How...or why...would God not avail Himself of smarter and more talented individuals than me? The answer appeared in my doorway one morning.

Gina knocked lightly to grab my attention. In our short time working together, we forged a friendship founded on our different personalities. Her people-focused, creative style complemented my serious, results-oriented leadership. She challenged me to connect with hearts when I focused on engaging minds. She pushed me to step into fun and unpredictable antics, while I preferred giving rein to my reserved, poised nature. Yet not everyone in our buttoned-downed financial world recognized Gina's gift to draw out the creative side of others.

After quietly shutting the door, Gina presented to me a beautifully wrapped gift. "It's unusual," she headlined. "I'll explain once you open it."

The bow and paper fell away to reveal a snow globe music box situated on a round pedestal-shaped stage. Inside the globe, a ballerina sat on a soft-cushioned stool, readying herself to dance. I gave the globe a shake, and snow fell gently around the ballerina to the tune of "Swan Lake." The gift touched me, but what made Gina think of me when she saw it?

Gina reached over and gingerly took hold of the globe. "This is how you make me feel," she began. "When we work together, you let

me be whatever and however I want to be. You never try to change who I am." She paused and then whispered, "You let me dance."

The Spirit nudged, "Gloria, *this* is your purpose. You don't have to be a financial whiz here. Only give from what I gave *you*."

I did not need a finance degree or experience to complete my God-given assignments at a financial organization. Instead, He gave me a scholarship and training for my master's in social work. He equipped me with counseling and coaching skills. He gave me a passion for helping others realize their full potential. And that is all I needed to achieve His purpose wherever He planted me.

CONNECTING THE DOTS

Give what we can. Give all we can. Lead with that wherever God plants us and with whoever He plants in our path. Expect God to connect the dots and fill the gaps.

God gives each of us different abilities, gifts, and strengths (Romans 12:6). When He then calls us to a moment or season, in a place or to a person, He expects us to give only from what He has given us. Nothing more. Nothing less. He never asks us to give what we don't have to give or do what we don't have the capability to do.

Though we may initially hesitate at where or how God calls us, the Lord provides *all* we need. If we lack something, then we don't need it to complete what He wants us to do. We need only give what He entrusted to us for the purpose of helping someone dance their "Swan Lake."

> *Now a man crippled from birth was being carried to the temple gate called Beautiful, where he was put every day to beg from those going into the temple courts. When he saw Peter and John about to enter, he asked them for money... Peter said, "Silver and gold I do not have, but what I have, I give you. In the name of Jesus Christ of Nazareth, walk."*
> Acts 3:2-6 (NIV)

66

ACT 3, SCENE 1 – PIERCED

· · · · · · · · ● ● ◉ ● ● · · · · · · ·

Pierced. What kind of word is that for God to give me to guide my life through the coming year? Yet, that's the word the Holy Spirit repeatedly laid upon my heart in 2018.

When I looked up *pierced* in the dictionary, nothing attractive or comforting jumped out. I saw definitions like…

> *…to penetrate; stab*
> *…to make a hole in or through; to perforate; to riddle with numerous openings*
> *…to sound sharply through (such as a shriek pierced the air)*

Synonyms left even less to be desired … *pungent, agonizing, intense, cutting, painful, and poignant.* Surely, I misunderstood. There must be static on my spirit's connection with His. I wanted a word that would grow and deepen my faith. I prayed again and listened … no, hoped for … a word with less pain involved, thank you very much.

Then, the piercings began. Piercings that punctured my dreams and visions of retired life. Perforated holes that riddled my self-worth and identity, leaving empty voids.

The first pierce came in January. I handed over — willingly, mind you — leadership reins to Christian Women's Connection.[4] I stepped into this role as chairperson the day I retired, thus transitioning from a full-time paid job to a full-time volunteer one.

Without skipping a beat from corporate America, the day-to-day routine filled my time with organizing monthly programs, coordinating the planning team, and selecting speakers. I met and encouraged upcoming leaders, set up a webpage, created a newsletter, and wrote blogs to keep participants connected.

Although ready to pass the baton, for the first time in 40 years, I held no title to put on a business card; no position or role as director, vice-president, or leader of any kind to give me identity and purpose. *What goals will I work toward now?*

Before I could catch my breath from the pain of that piercing, the second one struck. On February 1, the phone rang, shaking me awake from a nap. Although caller ID said my friend was giving me a buzz, the voice I heard was her husband's.

"Gloria, I'm so sorry to tell you this," he said as his voice caught with a sob. "Leah Jane passed away this morning. She collapsed, and we could not revive her."

My friend's death closed a chapter in my life that lasted 35 plus years. It erased regular lunches and phone calls we shared to mark the milestones in our lives and that of our families.

Months of additional losses followed.

A letter asking forgiveness went unanswered and red-lined my hope for restoration of the relationship.

Unexpected family situations and responsibilities consumed another close friend with whom I once spent hours planning and sharing in outreach ministries.

A daughter who announced that she and her husband were selling everything in exchange for life on the road in a 40-foot motor home, *indefinitely*. She never lived more than 50 miles from us, even during college years. They left in August and took with them my vision of grandparenting romps and snuggles with our two young granddaughters. Our weekly Saturday routine came to an abrupt halt.

I felt like my writer's group grabbed ahold of my life and was drawing a line through whole paragraphs, adjectives, and adverbs that once defined my storyline. While those fellow authors intended their edits to make my story stronger, these red-lined entries left me wondering if I had any story left to tell.

The final agonizing cut came in September. Out of the blue, my husband announced we needed to move our church membership. The time had come, according to him, to shift from the congregation seven miles from our home to the local, smaller one.

"Say what??" I argued, "Do you mean leave the one where I've spent the last five years building relationships and teaching Bible studies? The church that is my last link to any semblance of a leadership role? Where I spent the last two years helping the associate pastor build a Path to Discipleship for the congregation? Are you asking me to leave *that* church?"

My husband's one-word answer, "Yes."

One month later, after discussions with spouse and toe-in-the-water visits to the proposed church, we began to attend worship with the local congregation two miles and five minutes from our home.

2018, indeed, pierced and left me riddled with holes in my portfolio of purposeful work. My stock value, from my vantage point, dropped with every edit. I wondered, *what good am I now?*

· · · · · 🖋 · · · · ·

The answer came slowly like the morning haze of a fog that clears away with the noonday sun.

On January 1, 2018, I had journaled two verses using my Spirit-given word, *pierced.* The first said,

*...the word of God is living and active, sharper than any two-edged sword, **piercing** until it divides soul from spirit, joints from marrow; it is able to judge the thoughts and intentions of the heart.*
Hebrews 4:12 (NRSV)

Commentary on this verse guided me to a second in which God laid out for the Israelites a law concerning slaves:

When you buy a male Hebrew slave, he shall serve six years, but in the seventh he shall go out a free person, without debt... But if the slave declares, "I love my master, my wife, and my children; I will not go out a free person," then his master shall bring him before God. He shall be brought to the door or the doorpost; and his master shall pierce his ear with an awl; and he shall serve him for life.
Exodus 21:2, 5-6 (NRSV)

On the same day, I journaled the commitment these verses pressed on my heart:

I choose Christ as my master for life. In 2018, may His words, promptings and circumstances pierce my heart...

...to mold me closer to His image.

...to lead me wherever.

...to create openings through which His light might shine through my life.

...all that I might know Him better and follow Him more closely.

As I reflected on my new year's commitment, the awl of God's words pierced my spiritual eyes and ears. Unwittingly, I allowed other things to keep me from making *Him* the priority and master of my life. The edits pierced through the defenses and self-interests on which I had come to rely for self-worth.

As 2018 marched to an end and 2019 came into view, I let go of mourning the year of piercings and began to bathe instead in the morning comfort of God's presence.

CONNECTING THE DOTS

Embrace a pierced life.

While sometimes painful, that kind of season allows more abundant opportunity for God to penetrate our awareness of His presence and unconditional love. And, a life riddled with piercings also creates more openings. Those openings create more time and availability, through which God's light in us can shine through to the world.

Stay tuned. Even when we are obeying and producing good in our activities and relationships, a time may come when God prunes even that branch of our life so that we can bear even more good fruit.

Jesus said, I am the Real Vine and my Father is the Farmer. He cuts off every branch of me that doesn't bear grapes. And every branch that is grape-bearing he prunes back so it will bear even more.
John 15:2 (The Message)

67

ACT 3, SCENE 2 – MOURNING TO MORNING

· · · · · · · · ● ● ● ◉ ● ● ● ● ● · · · ·

I mourned each piercing life-edit of 2018. Wallowing in exhaustion, and with more years behind me than ahead, I identified with the prophet Elijah, *Enough of this, God! Take my life – I'm ready to join my ancestors in the grave!* (1 Kings 19:5, The Message)

Elijah had defeated and slain 450 Baal prophets with fire from heaven – a mountaintop experience with God. Events then took a surprise turn. Queen Jezebel swore vengeance upon Elijah, and he ran for his life. Courage left him; despondency reared its ugly head, as it now did with me.

I despaired the piercings and prunings from my life. How could my too-old, too-insignificant self make much difference any longer? Avenues of influence were absent.

Despite still counting many blessings – a loving and faithful husband, my health and that of family, and a roof over my head in my dream home – I mourned the loss of a role to play that I deemed gave me value. I felt too small to count.

One fall day, at the dining room table of Pat, a dear friend, the conversation triggered my tears as I laid open my heart. I ended my tale of woe on a sniffle and a question, "What good am I now?"

Without saying a word, Pat rose from her chair, walked to her kitchen drawer, and pulled out a ¼ teaspoon measuring spoon.

She placed the ¼ teaspoon in my hand and said, "Remember the story you told women at the retreat a few years back – the one about making cornbread. You didn't have the ¼ teaspoon of baking powder the recipe called for. So, thinking it was too small to count, you left it out. What you baked was a hockey puck of cornbread."

> ...God nourished and re-energized me for the next assignments. He turned my whining to wining on His Word.

She paused and then reminded me of my lesson, "*No one* is too small to count. Each person and ingredient counts."

Pat took my hand and looked me in the eyes. "Gloria, all you can do is bring your ¼ teaspoon of whatever God gives you in every situation each day. You may not be the big stuff – the cornmeal, the eggs, or the milk. But your ¼ tsp may be the catalyst, just like the baking powder, to make everything rise up."

Isn't it maddening when your own words come back to haunt you?

CONNECTING THE DOTS

God nourishes and equips us with what we need to face what lies ahead.

With my friend's words, the house lights came up on my life's Act 3, Scene 2. Mourning turned to morning. My story was not finished.

God still planned a purpose for me. But, for now, He awarded me an intermission, a pause, a rest in between scenes before He sent me in a different direction.

For the next six months, like Elijah, God nourished and re-energized me for the next assignments. He turned my whining to wining on His Word. Now clear of old sources of strength and confidence, God had space to reveal – yet again – that He was, is, and will be my truest Rock. In the words of an old-time favorite hymn, *He is the Rock on whom I stand; all other ground is sinking sand.*

Suddenly, an angel shook him [Elijah] awake and said, "Get up and eat!" ...The angel of God came back, shook him awake again, and said, "Get up and eat some more – you've got a long journey ahead of you."
1 Kings 19:5, 7 (The Message)

68

AGE LIKE THE OLIVE TREE

A ten-day pilgrimage turned the page to my life's next chapter.

As my season of life edits ended, I waited with time on my hands in between God-given assignments. While a young oldster who could still walk, I accepted a friend's offer to travel to Israel.

The trip's defining moment came on day two. In front of a tree.
An olive tree.
An olive tree in the Garden of Gethsemane.
Perhaps the very tree under which Jesus wept, agonized as I now did over the previous year's losses.

Standing by that tree did not turn the page. Rather, the olive tree's life story ushered in a revelation of what was really going on in this last chapter/act of my life.

Olive trees can live 5,000 plus years. The secret to their longevity is in their roots. They grow deep, are drought-tolerant, and flourish even in poor soil or rocky environments. Because they can survive harsh conditions, the olive tree often grows isolated from other plants. They also self-pollinate, leaving the olive tree less likely to succumb to genetic mutation or disease spread by other plants.

The olive tree's trunk and branches, however, do not live forever. Time, and occasionally disease, catches up with it. When they do, the inner bark deteriorates to ground level, hollowing out the tree trunk and leaving only the outer bark as a shell.

Despite the death of the tree's inner bark, the root system remains alive and strong. Roots sprout new shoots that grow from inside out, eventually forming a whole new olive tree. This process of the trunk dying and hollowing out to make room for new shoots can take place numerous times over the life of the tree.

In the Garden, I saw the dead and hollowed-out exterior of a 2,000 plus year-old olive tree. Its new trunk measured about six to eight inches in diameter and shot from the inside out into a canopy of new branches and green leaves.

In the Garden, Christ emptied/hollowed himself of all but His love for the Father. Those roots remained alive and strong. That's what the Father now asked of me in this next chapter of my life. To let go. To empty or hollow myself of comfortable roles, acquired statuses, satisfying assignments, even rewarding friendships …

All to make room for the new Gloria He wanted to grow from the inside out. I would still have the same outer appearance, though aging, but inside He was forming a new/transformed creation.

I already glimpsed new shoots. In Act 3, Scene 2, I was growing from retired and replaced to repurposed. From known and comfortable to unknown and vulnerable. From shedding finished roles, closing relationships, and completed assignments to sprouting new shoots of opportunity to which God called me.

CONNECTING THE DOTS

Don't put a period where God puts a comma. Age like the olive tree.

Our bodies and minds naturally grow older and slower with time. We can't do what we always did. Yet, if we sink our roots deeply into the Lord, He can and will still use us for His purposes.

Age in years does not matter. The hollowing out of the old only makes room for new sprouts to shoot from the inside out. Self-pollinating in the Spirit, we can grow where no others can. We can still produce good fruit for Him.

But I am like an olive tree flourishing in the house of
God; I trust in God's unfailing love forever and ever.
Psalm 52:8 (NIV)

69

TIPS ON GETTING
THE BEST RESULTS

More than first realized, the olive tree is a metaphor for how to live a long, prosperous life. Researching how best to plant and grow an olive tree yielded these four tips...and life lessons:

1. *Water daily and deeply the first month.* Afterwards, water them only once per month, thus forcing roots to grow deep and strong. Even though drought-tolerant, watering the olive tree is still necessary for abundant fruit production. No water = no growth or yields.

   Life Take-Away: Drink in God's Word regularly. Though we are drought-tolerant once deeply rooted in God's Word, His Word is still required for growth and production of good fruit. Reflect and meditate on it. See how it speaks to us and applies to daily life.

2. *Give olive trees at least seven hours of direct sunlight daily.* They require this much sunlight to thrive and produce.

   Life Take-Away: Walk in the light of the Son, Jesus Christ.

3. *Prune annually for abundant yields.* Remove only the branches that grow toward the center of the tree. This caretaking helps open the tree, allowing sunlight to access the fruit.

Life Take-Away: Work towards moving from a self-centered to a Spirit-centered life.

4. *Manage expectations for fruit.* Typically, olive trees grow slowly. Those planted in traditional open groves will not bear fruit until the fifth or sixth year. Full fruit production occurs around the seventh or eighth year. They reach peak production and yields between 65-80 years old. Then, fruit production progressively lessens for the rest of its life, even though it yields fruit for hundreds of years.

Life Take-Away: As we age, we often experience a slowing of our pace and capabilities. Yet, as Paul wrote to the Corinthians, "...do not lose heart. Even though our outer nature is wasting away, our inner nature is being renewed day by day" (2 Corinthians 4:16, NRSV). Translation: Don't think for a moment that we can't still produce something even in our senior years.

CONNECTING THE DOTS

Be patient and embrace aging. Our best production may come after years of God's nourishing us with His Word and equipping us with one experience after another.

The righteous will flourish like a palm tree, they will grow like a cedar of Lebanon; planted in the house of the LORD, they will flourish in the courts of our God. They will still bear fruit in old age; they will stay fresh and green...
Psalm 92:12-14 (NIV)

70

AGE TO PERFECTION

In my 20's and 30's, I viewed aging as falling apart. Now that I'm ... uhhhhh ... older, I connect the dots of truth differently. I see that God promised we would age to perfection. The proof was in my medical experiences one year.

The dentist said, "Gloria, you need a couple of crowns." After years of faithful brushing and flossing, I stared at him in disbelief. Insert heavy sigh and believe in God's truth:

> *He redeems me from death and crowns me*
> *with love and tender mercies.*
> Psalm 103:4 (NLT)

The receptionist from a potential internist floored me. After giving my information to set up an annual physical, she said, "I'm sorry, but the doctor doesn't accept patients your age." Insert catty remark. Doesn't she know God's truth?

The righteous will bear fruit in old age, they will stay fresh and green.
Psalm 92:14 (NIV)

The ophthalmologist completed my routine exam. "The bad news is you have the beginnings of a cataract. The good news is it probably won't cause a problem for fifteen years." Insert disappointing squint of my near-sighted eyes at him. Despite failing eyes, take comfort in God's truth:

Keep me as the apple of your eye.
Psalm 17:8a (NIV)

As I dragged my aging body out the last doctor's door, I squared my shoulders and adopted the motto from International Very Good-Looking, Dang Smart Woman's Day:[5]

Life should NOT be a journey to the grave with the intention of
arriving safely in an attractive and well-preserved body,
but rather to skid in sideways, chocolate in one hand,
wine in the other, body thoroughly used up,
totally worn out and screaming,
WOO HOO, what a ride!

CONNECTING THE DOTS

We all live in a body by God. Aging … and aged … to perfection in Him. When the enemy tries to use that reality to dash our self-image or crush our confidence, he will surely fail if we take our rightful position and stand our ground.

Learn to live a Word-shaped life. Face each day armed with the full armor of God, the first piece of which is the belt of His truth found in His Word.

Therefore, put on the full armor of God, so that when the day
of evil comes, you may be able to stand your ground, and after
you have done everything, to stand. Stand firm then, with the
belt of truth buckled around your waist with the breastplate
of righteousness in place, and with your feet fitted with the
readiness that comes from the gospel of peace. In addition to all

this, take up the shield of faith, with which you can extinguish all the flaming arrows of the evil one. Take the helmet of salvation and the sword of the Spirit, which is the word of God. ...
Ephesians 6:13-17 (NIV)

And be patient. Though outwardly our bodies are aging, inwardly, we are being perfected day by day (2 Corinthians 4:16). God is not yet finished with us on this side of heaven.

SECTION 8

·····❧·····

THE NEXT STEP

THE NEXT STEP

Let me be clear. I am not yet aged to perfection. My journey to fully living a Word-shaped life is not complete. I have more dots to connect every day. We all do.

God loves us and wants all of us to age to perfection; to experience life, abundant and eternal. Our problem is that we are lost. Like my wandering away from family at the beach, we choose to go our willful way. That choice separates us from God. As the Bible, His Word, says:

> *For all have sinned and fall short of the glory of God.*
> Romans 3:23, NIV

Our attempts to solve this problem is like playing a game of Whack-a-Mole...we try to correct one flaw or give up one vice only to see another pop up in how we are living. Or, in time or due to circumstances, we relapse into old ways.

Only one lasting solution exists, and that is Jesus Christ. God sent His only Son to pay the penalty of our sins once and for all. As a human, He faced, and so understands, our temptations and difficulties. Yet, He never sinned and lived in perfect communion with God, the Father. He died on the cross as the perfect sacrifice for our sins, and He rose from the dead. According to the Word:

> *God made him who had no sin to be sin for us,*
> *so that in him we might become the righteousness of God.*
> 2 Corinthians 5:21, NIV

> *But God demonstrates his own love for us in this:*
> *While we were still sinners, Christ died for us.*
> Romans 5:8, NIV

> *For the wages of sin is death, but the gift of God*
> *is eternal life in Christ Jesus our Lord.*
> Romans 6:23, NIV

God provided a way. A way for each of us to age to perfection and live in relationship with Him now and eternally.

> *But because of his great love for us, God, who is rich in*
> *mercy, made us alive with Christ even when we were dead*
> *in transgressions - it is by grace you have been saved.*
> Ephesians 2:4-5, NIV

But we must choose to receive this gift. How to do so is easy. As the first step, simply choose to receive Christ by praying this prayer:

> *Lord Jesus, I know that I am a sinner, and I ask for your forgiveness.*
> *I believe that you are the Son of God, and that you*
> *died for my sins and rose from the dead.*
> *I invite you to come into my heart and life.*
> *I want to trust and follow you as my Savior*
> *and as the Lord of my life.*
> *In your name, I pray, Amen.*

When you pray this prayer, God promises:

> *Everyone who calls on the name of the Lord shall be saved.*
> Romans 10:13 (NRSV)

By receiving Christ, you are now born into God's family through the supernatural work of the Holy Spirit who now dwells within you. This is what Jesus and the Bible call "new birth."

Now you are ready to connect the dots for yourself as the Holy Spirit leads you. To deepen your relationship with Christ:

1. Read and study the Bible daily to know Christ better as your friend.
2. Talk to God in prayer every day.
3. Worship in the fellowship of other Christian believers in a church where Christ is preached and followed.
4. Serve both inside and outside of the church in the name of Jesus Christ, according to the gifts, talents, and abilities that God has given you.
5. Be an ambassador for Christ with those who cross your path; take every opportunity to share the love of Christ that now lives in you.

May God bless you as you continue your lifelong journey, learning to live a Word-shaped life and aging to perfection.

Peace and Grace,
Gloria K. Ashby

NOTES

Introduction | Connecting the Dots

1. Oswald Chambers, "Why Cannot I Follow Thee Now?" *My Utmost for His Highest*, January 4.

Section 1 | Surrounded by a Great Cloud of Witnesses

1. First published in *Chicken Soup for the Soul: Grandmothers*, 2011, pp. 240-243.
2. www.Goodreads.com/quotes
3. A version of this story first appeared in *Bringing Hope: Life Changing Wisdom for Christ Followers*, by Liz Morris and the Dallas Dream Team.
4. Bill Peel and Walt Larimore, *Workplace Grace: Becoming a Spiritual Influence at Work*, LeTourneau University Press, 2014. p. 15.
5. Ibid, p. 21.
6. A version of this story first appeared in *Bringing Hope: Life Changing Wisdom for Christ Followers*, by Liz Morris and the Dallas Dream Team.

Section 2 | Life's Like That

1. Sperry, Neil. *Complete Guide to Texas Gardening*. Dallas: Taylor Publishing Company, 1982, p. 264.
2. Ibid, p. 269.
3. Author Unknown. Found on Thoughts-About-God.com.

SECTION 3 | SOMEBODY SHOULD'VE SAID SOMETHING

1. A version of this story first appeared in *Bringing Hope: Life Changing Wisdom for Christ Followers,* by Liz Morris and the Dallas Dream Team.
2. Two books that transformed my thinking and relationship with the Holy Spirit are *The Forgotten God: Reversing the Tragic Neglect of the Holy Spirit* by Frances Chan and *The Wonderful, Spirit-Filled Life* by Charles Stanley.
3. EmilyPost.com/advice accessed 5/25/2019.
4. First published as a devotional in *The Secret Place*, Spring, 2012.
5. This angel encounter happened to Debbie Johnson, my sister, who gave me written permission to write and include the story in this collection.
6. Goodreads.com/quotes.
7. Max Lucado, *God's Story, Your Story* p. 157.

SECTION 4 | LEARN TO LEAD LIKE JESUS

1. Chris O'Connell, "New Arrivals Prompt Penguins to Get Wet," *Los Angeles Times*, January 21, 2003.

SECTION 5 | FAITH WORDS TO GROW BY

1. A version of this story first appeared in *Bringing Hope: Life Changing Wisdom for Christ Followers,* by Liz Morris and the Dallas Dream Team.
2. Oxford Dictionaries, Online Bing Translator.
3. J. D. Walt, The Seedbed Daily Text, Seedbed.com; February 10, 2020.
4. Russell Kelso Carter, *Standing on the Promises*, The United Methodist Hymnal, p. 374.
5. Oxford Dictionaries, Online Bing Translator.
6. Ibid.
7. Ibid.

8. Ibid.
9. Ibid.
10. Ibid.
11. The Bible version shared was Max Lucado (General Editor), *The Devotional Bible: Experiencing the Heart of Jesus*, New Century Version, Thomas Nelson Bibles, 2003.
12. Oxford Dictionaries, Online Bing Translator.
13. Ibid.
14. Ibid.
15. Elizabeth Barrett Browning, from "Aurora Leigh."

SECTION 7 | AGING TO PERFECTION

1. J.D. Walt, "Trust God When the Way Seems Longer," *The Seedbed Daily Text*. March 25, 2020. Seedbed.com.
2. Many good inventories exist. I took the one by Charles V. Bryant, *Your Spiritual Gifts Inventory from Rediscovering Our Spiritual Gifts*, (Nashville: Upper room Books, 1997).
3. By "throw away" verse, I mean those scripture verses we might discard or slide over because we either don't want them or believe we don't need them to understand the message. However, if we will sit with them for a moment, we discover that they are rich in meaning. In themselves, they deliver a message we need to hear, a hidden truth we need to see.
4. Christian Women's Connection is associated with Stonecroft, a national women's ministry whose mission is to inspire women to reach other women with the gospel, each one where she is, as she is.
5. Author unknown.

SOURCES

Oswald Chambers, *My Utmost for His Highest.* Uhrichsville, Ohio: Barbour Publishing, Inc., 1963.

Mark Greene, *Fruitfulness on the Frontline: Making a Difference Where You Are.* Nottingham, England: Inter-Varsity Press, 2014.

James C. Howell, *The Kiss of God: 27 Lessons on the Holy Spirit.* Nashville: Abingdon Press, 2004.

Max Lucado, *God's Story, Your Story.* Grand Rapids, Michigan: Zondervan, 2011.

Chris O'Connell, "New Arrivals Prompt Penguins to Get Wet." *Los Angeles Times*, January 21, 2003.

Bill Peel and Walt Larimore, *Workplace Grace: Becoming a Spiritual Influence at Work.* Longview, Texas: LeTourneau University Press, 2014.

Neil Sperry, *Complete Guide to Texas Gardening.* Dallas: Taylor Publishing Company, 1982.

Oxford Dictionaries, Online Bing Translator.

United Methodist Hymnal, Nashville, Tennessee: The United Methodist Publishing House, 1989.

J. D. Walt, *Seedbed Daily Text.* Seedbed.com.

OTHER SOURCES
WORTH READING

These additional books both inspired and helped me connect the dots:

Henry Blackaby and Claude V. King. *Experiencing God: How to Live the Adventure of Knowing and Doing the Will of God*. Nashville: Broadman & Holman Publishers, 1994.

Brother Lawrence, *Practicing the Presence of God*. Nashville: Thomas Nelson Publishers, 1999.

Frances Chan, *The Forgotten God: Reversing the Tragic Neglect of the Holy Spirit*. Colorado Springs, Colorado: David C. Cook, 2009.

Disciple: Becoming Disciples Through Bible Study. Nashville: Abingdon Press, 2005.

Adam Hamilton. *Why? Making Sense of God's Will*. Nashville: Abingdon Press, 2011.

Adam Hamilton. *The Call: The Life and Message of the Apostle Paul*. Nashville: Abingdon Press, 2011.

John Ortberg, *If You Want to Walk on Water, You've Got to Get Out of the Boat*. Grand Rapids, Michigan: Zondervan, 2001.

John Ortberg, *The Me I Want to Be*. Grand Rapids, Michigan: Zondervan, 2010.

Priscilla Shirer, *Discerning the Voice of God: How to Recognize When God is Speaking*. Chicago: Moody Publishers, 2012.

Charles Stanley, *The Wonderful, Spirit-Filled Life*. Nashville: Thomas Nelson Publishers, 1992.

A.W. Tozer, *The Pursuit of God: The Human Thirst for the Divine*. Camp Hill, Pennsylvania: Christian Publications, 1993.

Dallas Willard, *Hearing God: Developing a Conversational Relationship with God*. Downers Grove, Illinois: InterVarsity Press, 1999.

SCRIPTURE REFERENCES

OT Genesis 28:15

OT Exodus 33:14

OT Numbers 9:17-20

OT Deuteronomy 6:12

OT Deuteronomy 7:8-9

OT Deuteronomy 31:7-8

OT 1 Kings 19: 5, 7

OT 2 Chronicles 33:12-13

OT Psalm 30:2-3, 5

OT Psalm 37:4-6

OT Psalm 52:8

OT Psalm 55:16-17

OT Psalm 91:11-12

OT Psalm 91:14-16

OT Psalm 105:4

OT Psalm 139:4-7

OT Proverbs 22:1

OT Proverbs 3:5-6

OT Ecclesiastes 3:11

OT Isaiah 55:10-11

OT Isaiah 55:11

OT Isaiah 6:8

OT Isaiah 41:10

OT Jeremiah 29:11

OT Lamentation 3:21-23

OT Obadiah 12, 15

OT Zechariah 4:10

NT Matthew 6:12, 14-15

NT Matthew 7:24-25

NT Matthew 13:31-32

NT Matthew 25:38

NT Mark 8:35-36

NT Mark 10:43

NT Luke 6:37-38

NT Luke 15:10

NT Luke 15:20

NT John 1:40-41

NT John 2:5

NT John 3:30

NT John 10:7-10

NT John 14:16

NT John 15:2

NT John 16:33

NT Acts 3:2-6

NT Acts 17:11

NT Acts 20:35

NT Romans 1:10

NT Romans 3:23

NT Romans 5:8

NT Romans 6:23

NT Romans 8:28

NT Romans 8:38-39

NT Romans 10:13

NT Romans 11:17-22

NT 1 Corinthians 12:16-18

NT 1 Corinthians 13:4-8

NT 1 Corinthians 15:58

NT 2 Corinthians 5:21

NT Galatians 3:3

NT Galatians 5:5

NT Ephesians 1:4-6

NT Ephesians 2:4-5

NT Ephesians 2:10

NT Ephesians 4:16

NT Ephesians 4:32

NT Ephesians 6:13-14

NT Philippians 1:4-6

NT Philippians 2:3-4

NT Philippians 2:13

NT Philippians 4:6-7

NT Philippians 4:8

NT Philippians 4:8-9

NT Colossians 3:1-2, 4

NT Colossians 3:12-14

NT Colossians 4:6

NT 1 Thessalonians 5:11

NT 1 Thessalonians 5:18

NT 1 Thessalonians 5:21

NT 2 Timothy 1:5-6

NT Hebrews 4:12-13

NT Hebrews 10:24-25

NT Hebrews 11:13-16

NT Hebrews 12:1-2

NT Hebrews 12:11

NT Hebrews 13:20-21

NT James 1:12

NT James 1:21

NT 1 Peter 3:1

NT 1 Peter 4:10

NT 1 Peter 5:10

ACKNOWLEDGEMENTS

No book comes together through a solo effort. Instead, a cloud of witnesses team up and encircle an individual to inspire, encourage, and support the project. *Connecting the Dots* is no exception.

The story began more than ten years ago over lunch with my daughter, Jessica Reyna. I owe her deep gratitude for helping my dream to take flight that day. All I wanted to do was speak and share my stories. Her public relations and communications experience pushed me to write so that I might speak.

Next came a myriad of writer's groups like Christian Communicators with Vonda Skelton and critique groups hosted by Frank Ball. Thank you for raising the bar on my writing and speaking skills. Your invaluable wisdom continues to push me to "show, not tell" my story and keep it advancing.

Similar thanks go to Donna Skell of Roaring Lambs Ministries. Your voice echoes to me as I write, saying "When your presentation is over, who will they remember … you or Jesus?" My hope is that my readers and listeners remember Jesus and His great love. Thank you for reminding me of the true measure of success.

This journey to publishing might have ended earlier except for those who encouraged me to keep going. Thank you to Pat Gordon, my long-time friend and frequent co-facilitator. I treasure the ministry moments we share, your listening ear to my doubts and fears, and holding me accountable with honesty and gentleness as an "ambassador for Christ." I appreciate my friends like Liz Morris and The Dallas Dream Team as well as Sage Appleby of Stonecroft Ministries. Thank you both for turning up the heat on the flame of my passion for reaching the lost and for giving me forums through which to serve.

I give heartfelt thanks to my sister Debbie Johnson. You always challenge me with questions and debates about practical application of scripture to life experiences. You also serve as a role model – the Mary, who knows how to sit and "be," to my Martha, who runs around to "do" and gets upset when others don't. You teach me that balance.

This book would still be collecting dust in a three-ring binder if it were not for my publisher, Mary Eckard. Thank you, my friend, for the hours you spent editing, suggesting, and pointing me in the right direction for navigating the self-publishing process. Your wisdom and experience saved me from hours of frustration and rework. Your encouragement spurred me onward to believe the dream was possible.

And I owe a special thanks to Jim, my husband. You have been my solid rock, the one on whom I leaned most heavily while laboring through this process. A generous giver of your time and resources, I can't count the number of cups of tea you poured or bowls of soup you heated when I was too intent on writing to stop for a break. Thank you, too, for reading every story and correcting my faulty memory around dates and places. If not for your love and patience, only fragments of these stories would exist and be gathering dust in my mind.

Finally, my greatest thanks to God, my Father and Creator. I thank You, my Lord and Savior, with my whole being for helping me connect the dots; for my hopefully becoming a better dot along the way; and for showing me how to live a Word-shaped life. To You I owe and give all the praise and glory.

MEET GLORIA

Gloria has spent a lifetime in pursuit of God and a Word-shaped life. She connects the dots for herself and others by teaching, leading Bible studies, and mentoring in both secular and faith-based settings. Her passion is to be an ambassador for Christ, sharing His Word and encouraging others to realize their full potential as children of our God and Creator.

In addition to authoring numerous inspirational stories found in *Chicken Soup for the Soul* and other devotionals, Gloria co-authored with Roaring Lambs Ministries the workbook, *My Story for God's Glory: Telling What He Has Done for Me.*

Gloria holds an undergraduate degree in Religious Education and Secondary Education, and a master's degree in Social Work. She and her husband, Jim, live in Texas. When not teaching, you can find her spending leisure mornings over scripture with a cup of hot tea, reading Christian fiction or a good mystery, tending her butterfly garden, and enjoying a game of mahjongg or canasta with friends. Gloria is the proud mom of one married daughter and two precious granddaughters who keep their Gigi and Grandpa Jim hopping.

Gloria would love to hear how this book impacted or resonated with you. To connect with her, or if you would like to schedule Gloria to speak at your event, please contact her at gloriaashby.connectingdots@gmail.com.

Made in the USA
Middletown, DE
11 February 2021